# Ed[illegible]gh

HarperCollins*Publishers*

# YOUR COLLINS TRAVELLER

**Your Collins Traveller Guide will help you find your way around your chosen destination quickly and easily. It is colour-coded for easy reference:**

**The blue section** answers the question 'I would like to see or do something; where do I go and what do I see when I get there?' This section is arranged as an alphabetical list of topics. Within each topic you will find:

- A selection of the best examples on offer.
- How to get there, costs and opening hours for each entry.
- The outstanding features of each entry.
- A simplified map, with each entry plotted and the nearest landmark or transport access.

**The red section** is a lively and informative gazetteer. It offers:

- Essential facts about the main places and cultural items. What is La Bastille? Who was Michelangelo? Where is Delphi?

**The gold section** is full of practical and invaluable travel information. It offers:

- Everything you need to know to help you enjoy yourself and get the most out of your time away, from Accommodation through Baby-sitters, Car Hire, Food, Health, Money, Newspapers, Taxis, Telephones to Youth Hostels.

**Cross-references:**

Type in small capitals – CHURCHES – tells you that more information on an item is available within the topic on churches.

**A-Z** after an item tells you that more information is available within the gazetteer. Simply look under the appropriate name.

A name in bold – **Holy Cathedral** – also tells you that more information on an item is available in the gazetteer – again simply look up the name.

# CONTENTS

# CONTENTS

Leith

Cecil B. De Mille could not have designed a better set for one of his epics. Edinburgh Castle, sitting proudly on its rock, dominates the city as it looks down on the elegance of the New Town and the rugged timelessness of the Old Town. However, for all this grandeur, Edinburgh is a charming place which retains a small town feel.

The sense of history is almost palpable. Wander down the winding streets and cobbled closes of the Old Town and you may almost expect to meet a medieval housewife going about her business only a stone's throw away from modern-day living and glaring souvenir shops. Yet Edinburgh's very beginnings are difficult to trace.

By the 5thC Pictish tribes had occupied the castle rock and realized its defensive potential. Other conquerors followed but the city's destiny was assured when Malcolm Canmore moved his court there from Dunfermline in the 11thC. Thereafter Edinburgh flourished.

At the heart of the city is the castle which houses a military museum and the Scottish Regalia. On a clear day the view from the esplanade over the city and the outlying area is spectacular. At one o'clock every day local people can be spotted checking their watches as a gun is fired from the artillery platform. Each year the esplanade is also used for the Military Tattoo, an extravaganza featuring bands and display teams from all over the world. The sight and sound of the massed pipes and drums on a chilly September night will never be forgotten.

By the 16thC most of the Old Town had been built and the street names of today point to their earlier use. The Lawnmarket was where cloth was sold; the Grassmarket was the place for agricultural products, and Candlemaker Row is self-explanatory!

In contrast to these streets is the elegant New Town. In the 18thC the city's officials decided the time had come for expansion and a competition was held to find a designer. The winner was an unknown 23-year-old architect, James Craig. His plan was classic and grand and the results can be seen today in the beautiful streets which are his legacy.

To gain a better idea of life for the wealthy inhabitants of Edinburgh at the time, visit the Georgian House in Charlotte Square which has been lovingly restored by the National Trust for Scotland. There is furniture in the style of Sheraton and Chippendale, porcelain by Wedgewood and paintings by Ramsay.

Waverley
market
Speciality shopping

Although the sense of history is ever-present Edinburgh has not stood still. After World War II a major arts event was mooted and out of that was born the annual International Festival, first held in 1947. At the end of August and in early September it attracts leading companies from all over the world. There are plays, reviews, mimes, recitals and operas. As if that were not enough there are also Fringe events. And with a Jazz Festival and a Film Festival also taking place during this period the choice is staggering.

In other fields too, Edinburgh has excelled. It takes a leading role in the banking and financial world, its university is renowned – especially for the teaching of science and medicine – and the major law courts of Scotland are in the city. Although Dr Johnson once wrote that the best sight for a Scotsman was the road to England, the converse is now true. Increasingly, people from the South are making their way north, attracted by living in a place where the quality of life is hard to match in other British cities.

For the tourist, however, the problem remains not what to see and do but how to choose what to leave for another visit. Away from the galleries, the museums and the Palace of Holyroodhouse, there are the shops. Rightly, Princes Street is well known. Its setting is unrivalled but unfortunately the majority of its shops are now chain stores, the one

exception being Jenners, which offers a wide range of traditional and high-quality goods. In many of the side streets there are small individual shops and if you are interested in taking home some history the antique shops in St. Stephen Street should prove interesting.

If you tire of the city itself, there are many villages nearby worth visiting. Probably one of the most picturesque is Cramond. The Cramond Inn is a popular stopping-off point and Cramond House is said to have been the setting for Robert Louis Stevenson's House of Shaws in *Kidnapped*. However, the village nestling around the River Almond estuary is worthwhile just for a stroll.

There are also many pubs and restaurants to relax in during the evening after a day's sightseeing. Leith is fast becoming the Covent Garden of Edinburgh and Rose Street, behind Princes Street, has long been renowned for the number of pubs along it. Many have tried to have a drink in each one of a night – few have succeeded!

For history, atmosphere and sheer enjoyment there are few places that will reward the visitor as well as this proud capital.

ADY STAIR'S HOUSE
A CITY MUSEUM

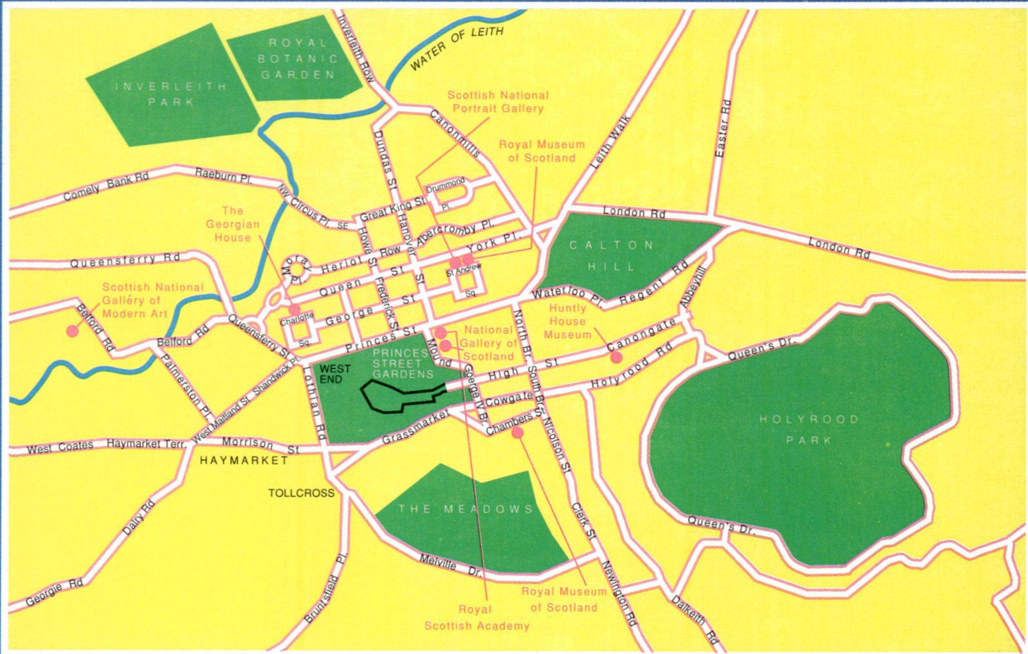
INVERLEITH PARK
ROYAL BOTANIC GARDEN
WATER OF LEITH
Inverleith Row
Scottish National Portrait Gallery
Royal Museum of Scotland
Leith Walk
Easter Rd
Canonmills
Dundas St
Comely Bank Rd
Raeburn Pl.
NW Circus Pl.
SE
Great King St
Drummond Pl.
Hanover St
Abercromby Pl.
York Pl.
Howe St
Row
Heriot
Moray Pl.
St Andrew Sq.
The Georgian House
Queensferry Rd
Queen St
Frederick St
George St
Charlotte Sq.
London Rd
CALTON HILL
Regent Rd
Waterloo Pl.
Abbeyhill
Scottish National Gallery of Modern Art
Belford Rd
Belford Rd
Queensferry St
Princes St
Mound
National Gallery of Scotland
North Br.
Huntly House Museum
Canongate
Queen's Dr.
PRINCES STREET GARDENS
WEST END
High St
Holyrood Rd
Palmerston Pl.
Shandwick Pl.
Lothian Rd
George IV Br.
Cowgate
South Br.
HOLYROOD PARK
West Maitland St
Grassmarket
Chambers St
Nicolson St
West Coates
Haymarket Terr.
Morrison St
HAYMARKET
TOLLCROSS
THE MEADOWS
Clerk St
Queen's Dr.
Dalry Rd
Melville Dr.
Georgie Rd
Bruntsfield Pl.
Royal Scottish Academy
Royal Museum of Scotland
Newington Rd
Dalkeith Rd

**NATIONAL GALLERY OF SCOTLAND** The Mound.
■ 1000-1700 Mon.-Sat., 1400-1700 Sun. ● Free.
*One of the best of Europe's small galleries. Collection of Impressionists.*

**ROYAL SCOTTISH ACADEMY** The Mound.
■ 1000-1900 Mon.-Sat., 1400-1700 Sun. ● £1.20, child 50p.
*Built in 1826 to Playfair's Greek temple design. Exhibitions of well-known foreign artists are held during the Edinburgh Festival* (*see* **A-Z**).

**ROYAL MUSEUM OF SCOTLAND** Chambers St.
■ 1000-1700 Mon.-Sat.,1400-1700 Sun. Bus 2, 3, 5, 7, 8, 21, 23, 27, 31, 33, 37, 41, 42, 46. ● Free.
*Displays of decorative arts, archaeology, ethnography, natural history, geology, technology and science. Lovely glass-roofed main hall.*

**ROYAL MUSEUM OF SCOTLAND** 1 Queen St.
■ 1000-1700 Mon.-Sat., 1400-1700 Sun. ● Free.
*Traces the history of Scotland from the Stone Age to modern times.*

**SCOTTISH NATIONAL PORTRAIT GALLERY** 1 Queen St.
■ 1000-1700 Mon.-Sat.,1400-1700 Sun. ● Free.
*Portraits of famous past Scots and the history of Scottish photography.*

**SCOTTISH NATIONAL GALLERY OF MODERN ART**
Belford Rd. ■ 1000-1700 Mon.-Sat., 1400-1700 Sun. Bus Eastern Scottish C13. ● Free.
*20thC art, including Hockney, Hepworth, Picasso and Moore.*

**HUNTLY HOUSE MUSEUM** 142 Canongate, Royal Mile.
■ 1000-1800 Mon.-Sat. (June-Sep.), 1400-1700 Sun. during the Festival; closes 1700 Oct.-Mar. Bus 1, 6. ● Free.
*Local history, pottery, shop signs, trade artefacts, etc. See* **WALK 1**.

**THE GEORGIAN HOUSE** 7 Charlotte Sq.
■ 1000-1700 Mon.-Sat., 1400-1700 Sun. (April-Nov.). ● £2.20.
*Georgian town house of c. 1800, lovingly restored. See* **WALK 2**.

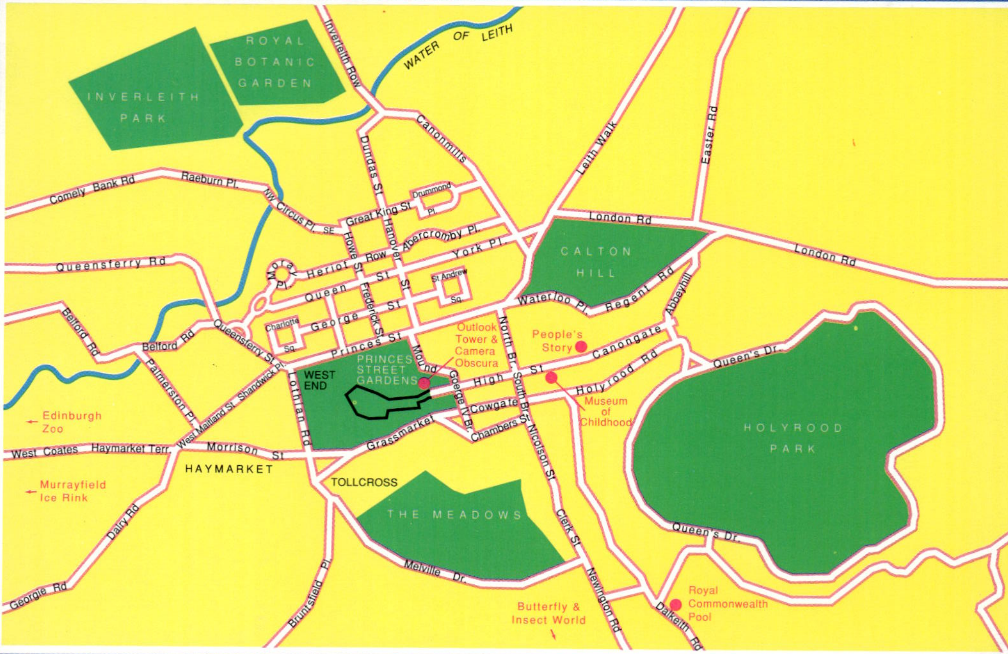

INVERLEITH PARK
ROYAL BOTANIC GARDEN
WATER OF LEITH
Inverleith Row
Canonmills
Leith Walk
Easter Rd
London Rd
CALTON HILL
Comely Bank Rd
Raeburn Pl.
NW Circus Pl.
SE
Great King St
Drummond Pl.
Dundas St
Hanover St
Howe St
Abercromby Pl.
York Pl.
Heriot Row
Queensferry Rd
Moray Pl.
Queen St
St Andrew Sq.
Frederick St
George St
Charlotte Sq.
Princes St
Waterloo Pl.
Regent Rd
Abbeyhill
Belford Rd
Queensferry St
Shandwick Pl.
Palmerston Pl.
West Maitland St
WEST END
PRINCES STREET GARDENS
Mound
Outlook Tower & Camera Obscura
North Br.
People's Story
Canongate
High St
Holyrood Rd
George IV Br.
Cowgate
Chambers St
South Br.
Nicolson St
Museum of Childhood
Queen's Dr.
HOLYROOD PARK
Lothian Rd
Grassmarket
Edinburgh Zoo
West Coates
Haymarket Terr.
Morrison St
HAYMARKET
TOLLCROSS
Murrayfield Ice Rink
Dalry Rd
THE MEADOWS
Clerk St
Queen's Dr.
Melville Dr.
Newington Rd
Gorgie Rd
Bruntsfield Pl.
Butterfly & Insect World
Royal Commonwealth Pool
Dalkeith Rd

**MUSEUM OF CHILDHOOD** 42 High St, Royal Mile.
■ 1000-1800 Mon.-Sat. (June-Sep.), 1400-1700 Sun. during the Festival; closes 1700 Oct.-Mar. Bus 1, 6, 34, 35. ● Free.
*Toys, dolls, games and all the paraphernalia of childhood through the ages. See* **WALK 1**.

**EDINBURGH ZOO** Corstorphine Rd. ■ 0900-1800 Mon.-Sat., 0930-1800 Sun. Bus 2, 12, 26, 31, 85, 86. ● £3.75, child £2.
*The zoo is famous for its colony of penguins, which parade daily in summer. See* **A-Z**.

**PEOPLE'S STORY** Canongate Tolbooth, 163 Canongate.
■ 1000-1800 Mon.-Sat. (June-Sep.), 1400-1700 Sun. during the Festival; closes 1700 Oct.-Mar. Bus 1, 6, 34, 35. ● Free.
*Shows the daily life of local citizens through the ages. See* **WALK 1**.

**OUTLOOK TOWER & CAMERA OBSCURA** Royal Mile.
■ 1000-1800 April-Oct., 1000-1700 Nov.-Mar. Bus 1, 6, 23, 27, 30, 34, 35, 40, 41, 42, 46. ● £2.50, child £1.25.
*An optical system which projects a live image of the city, plus displays of holography and pinhole cameras. See* **WALK 1**.

**BUTTERFLY & INSECT WORLD** Dobbie's Gardening World, Lasswade. ■ 1000-1730 April-Oct. Bus LRT 3, Eastern Scottish 80, 80A from St. Andrew Sq. ● £2.60, child £1.45.
*Glasshouse with tropical plants, butterflies, stick insects, scorpions, etc.*

**ROYAL COMMONWEALTH POOL** 21 Dalkeith Rd.
■ 0900-2100 Mon.-Fri., 1000-1600 Sat. & Sun. Bus 2, 12, 21, 33, 82, 83. ● £1 for pool, £1 for waterslides.
*Exciting enclosed waterslides built onto swimming pool complex.*

**MURRAYFIELD ICE RINK** Riversdale Cres.
■ 1430-1630. Bus 2, 12, 26. ● £1.20 plus 50p skate hire.
*Ice-skating is very popular in Scotland and the Murrayfield rink is the ideal place to try your skill. Tuition is available.*

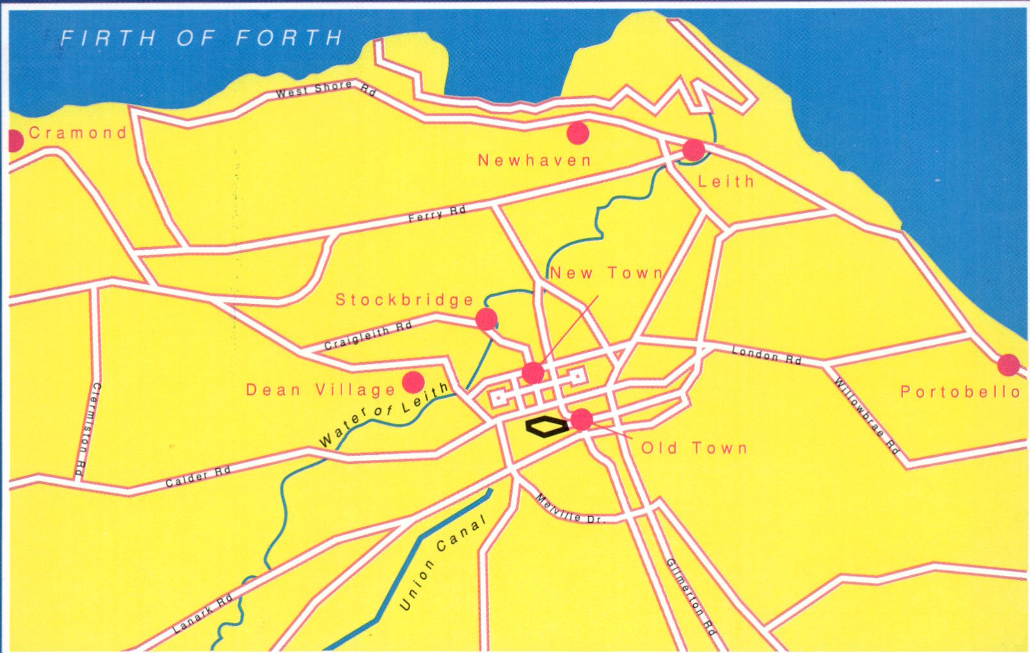
FIRTH OF FORTH
Cramond
West Shore Rd
Newhaven
Leith
Ferry Rd
New Town
Stockbridge
Craigleith Rd
Dean Village
Water of Leith
London Rd
Portobello
Willowbrae Rd
Old Town
Clermiston Rd
Calder Rd
Melville Dr.
Union Canal
Lanark Rd
Gilmerton Rd

**OLD TOWN** *Tall tenement buildings, many dating from the 15th-17thC, and narrow closes characterize Edinburgh's atmospheric Old Town. See* **WALK 1**, **A-Z**.

**NEW TOWN** *Built 1767-1840 to relieve overcrowding in the Old Town. Broad streets and sweeping terraces, spacious gardens and elegant Georgian architecture combine to create the classical beauty of the New Town. See* **WALK 2**, **A-Z**.

**DEAN VILLAGE** *(Bus 41 to Dean Bridge, then walk down Bell's Brae.) A picturesque village, dating from the 12thC, that grew up around the mills on the Water of Leith. See* **WALK 4**.

**LEITH** *(Bus 2, 9, 10, 12, 16, 22, 25, 34, 35, 87, 89.) For centuries Leith has been the Scottish capital's seaport. Now it is a fashionable area with new restaurants and wine bars springing up along the waterfront.*

**STOCKBRIDGE** *(Bus 24, 28, 29, 34, 35, 41A.) No more than a rural hamlet until the 18thC, when it was enveloped by the growing city, Stockbridge retains a village atmosphere with its busy shops and tea-rooms huddled around the bridge over the Water of Leith. See* **WALK 4**.

**PORTOBELLO** *(Bus 2, 12, 15, 26, 42, 46, 85, 86, 89.) Dating from the mid-18thC, Portobello was Victorian Edinburgh's seaside resort, with bracing sea air and miles of golden sands. The promenade, beach and amusements still draw plenty of summer visitors today.*

**NEWHAVEN** *(Bus 9, 10, 11, 16, 22.) Rows of cottages cluster behind Newhaven Harbour in this former fishing village. It supplied the city with oysters and herring in the 18th and 19thC. There is a local museum in Victoria School, Main St.*

**CRAMOND** *(Bus 18, 41.) A picture-postcard village at the mouth of the River Almond on the west edge of the city. It was once a busy industrial area based on milling grain and making iron, paper and cloth. A popular spot for weekend picnickers and strollers.*

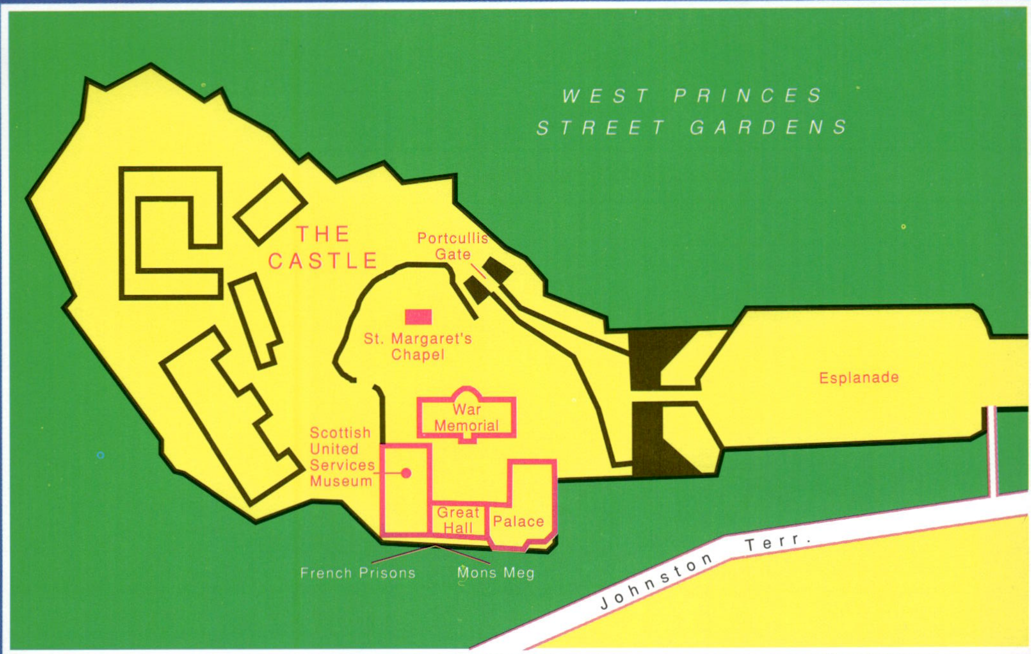
WEST PRINCES
STREET GARDENS
THE
CASTLE
Portcullis
Gate
St. Margaret's
Chapel
War
Memorial
Scottish
United
Services
Museum
Great
Hall
Palace
French Prisons
Mons Meg
Esplanade
Johnston Terr.

The castle entrance is at the top of the Royal Mile (see **A-Z**).
■ 0930-1705 Mon.-Sat., 1100-1705 Sun. (April-Sep.); 0930-1620 Mon.-Sat.,1230-1535 Sun. (Oct.-Mar.) Closed Jan. 1-4. Bus 1, 6, 23, 27, 30, 34, 35, 40, 41, 42, 46, 89. ● £2.80, child £1.40, family £4.

**ESPLANADE & GATEHOUSE** *The Esplanade (built in 1753) is the setting for the Military Tattoo. The Gatehouse is Victorian, built 1882-88. The statues are of Robert the Bruce and William Wallace.*

**PORTCULLIS GATE & MILLS MOUNT BATTERY** *The gate stands on the site of the 14thC Constable's Tower, and dates from 1577, although it was rebuilt in 1867. The Battery overlooks Princes St, and it is from here that the One o'Clock Gun (see* **A-Z***) is fired each day.*

**ST. MARGARET'S CHAPEL** *The city's oldest surviving building, dating from the 11thC, occupies the highest point of the Castle Rock. It was built by David I, son of the saintly Queen Margaret, in 1097.*

**SCOTTISH UNITED SERVICES MUSEUM**
■ 0930-1230, 1400-1700 Mon.-Sat., 1230-1630 Sun. ● Free.
*Covers the history of the armed forces in Scotland.*

**THE GREAT HALL** *This splendid hall, built at the order of James IV in the 16thC, sits on top of the French Prisons. There is fine wood-panelling, displays of weapons and armour, and a hammer-beam roof.*

**THE FRENCH PRISONS** *These gloomy dungeons, deep in the vaults below the Great Hall, held French prisoners during the Napoleonic Wars. Graffiti written by the unfortunate inmates can still be seen on the walls.*

**MONS MEG** *A magnificent siege cannon dating from c.1440, and once capable of firing 330 lb cannonballs at targets up to 1750 yd away.*

**THE PALACE** *This 16thC palace was the royal residence before the completion of Holyroodhouse (see* **A-Z***) at the far end of the Royal Mile. It is now the home of the Scottish Regalia – Crown, Sword and Sceptre.*

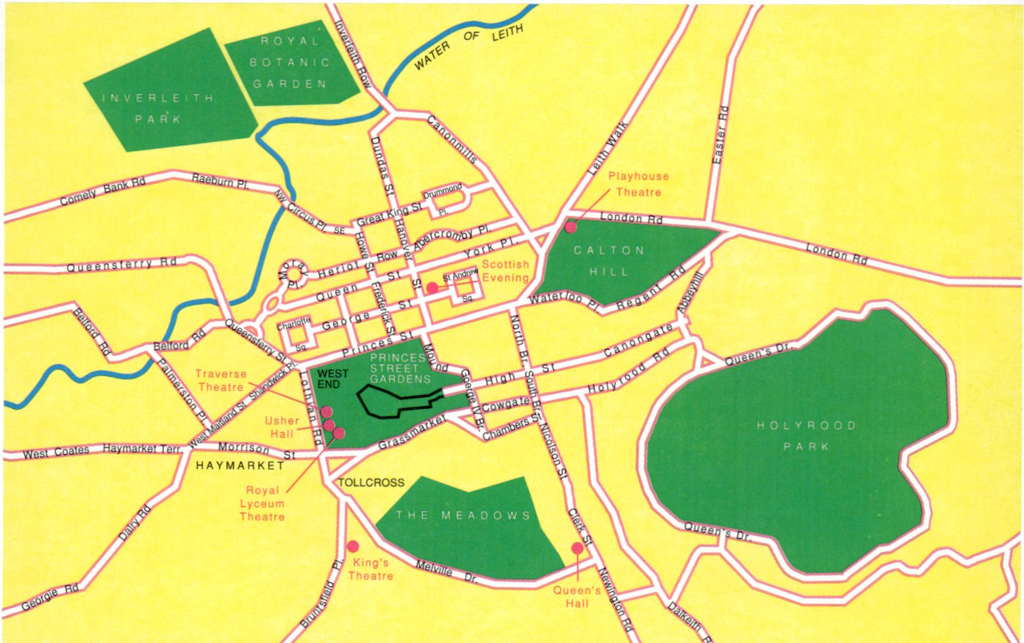
ROYAL BOTANIC GARDEN
INVERLEITH PARK
WATER OF LEITH
Inverleith Row
Canonmills
Leith Walk
Easter Rd
Playhouse Theatre
London Rd
London Rd
CALTON HILL
Regent Rd
Abbeyhill
Waterloo Pl.
Scottish Evening
St Andrew Sq.
York Pl.
Abercromby Pl.
Drummond Pl.
Great King St
Dundas St
Hanover St
Howe St
Heriot Row
Raeburn Pl.
Comely Bank Rd
NW Circus Pl.
SE
Moray Pl.
Queensferry Rd
Queen St
Frederick St
George St
Charlotte Sq.
Princes St
Belford Rd
Belford Rd
Queensferry St
Shandwick Pl.
PRINCES STREET GARDENS
WEST END
Mound
George IV Br.
High St
Canongate
Holyrood Rd
Cowgate
Chambers St
North Br.
South Br.
Nicolson St
Clerk St
Newington Rd
Queen's Dr.
Queen's Dr.
HOLYROOD PARK
Traverse Theatre
Usher Hall
Lothian Rd
Grassmarket
Royal Lyceum Theatre
Palmerston Pl.
West Maitland St
West Coates
Haymarket Terr.
Morrison St
HAYMARKET
TOLLCROSS
THE MEADOWS
Melville Dr.
King's Theatre
Bruntsfield Pl.
Queen's Hall
Dalkeith Rd
Dalry Rd
Georgie Rd

**ROYAL LYCEUM THEATRE** Grindlay St.
■ Box office 1000-1800 Mon.-Sat., tel: 2299697/7404. Bus 2, 9, 10, 11, 12, 15, 16, 18, 34, 35.
*The city's principal venue for drama. 1200-seat auditorium, built 1883.*

**PLAYHOUSE THEATRE** 18-21 Greenside Pl.
■ Box office 1000-1800 Mon.-Sat., tel: 5572590. Bus 4, 9, 10, 11, 15, 16, 22, 25, 34, 35, 42, 43, 44, 46.
*Scottish Opera, Scottish Ballet and big-name rock outfits can all be seen at this venue. There is a 3500-seat auditorium.*

**KING'S THEATRE** 2 Leven St.
■ Box office 1000-1800 Mon.-Sat., tel: 2291201/3416/4840. Bus 9, 10, 11, 16, 23, 27, 45, 47.
*Opera, ballet, drama, musicals, variety shows, Christmas pantomimes.*

**USHER HALL** Lothian Rd.
■ Box office 0900-1700 Mon.-Sat., tel: 2281155/1164. Bus 9, 10, 11, 15, 16, 18, 34, 35, 62.
*Lovely Victorian building, recently renovated. Classical concerts with the Scottish Chamber Orchestra and Royal Scottish Orchestra.*

**QUEEN'S HALL** 89 Clerk St.
■ Box office 1000-1700, tel: 6683456/2019. Bus 2, 3, 5, 7, 12, 24, 31, 33, 40, 41, 42, 46, 51.
*Regular classical, jazz, folk and pop concerts.*

**TRAVERSE THEATRE** Cambridge St.
■ Box office 1000-2000 Tue.-Sat., 1800-2200 Sun., tel: 2281404. Bus 2, 12, 23, 24, 27, 40, 41, 42, 45, 46.
*Famous theatre staging new works by Scottish and international writers.*

**SCOTTISH EVENING** George Hotel, 21 George St, tel: 2251251.
■ Shows 1915 Sun., Mon., Wed.-Fri. (April-Oct.) ● £29.50 inc. dinner.
*Traditional Scottish banquet with Highland dancing and accordion music.*

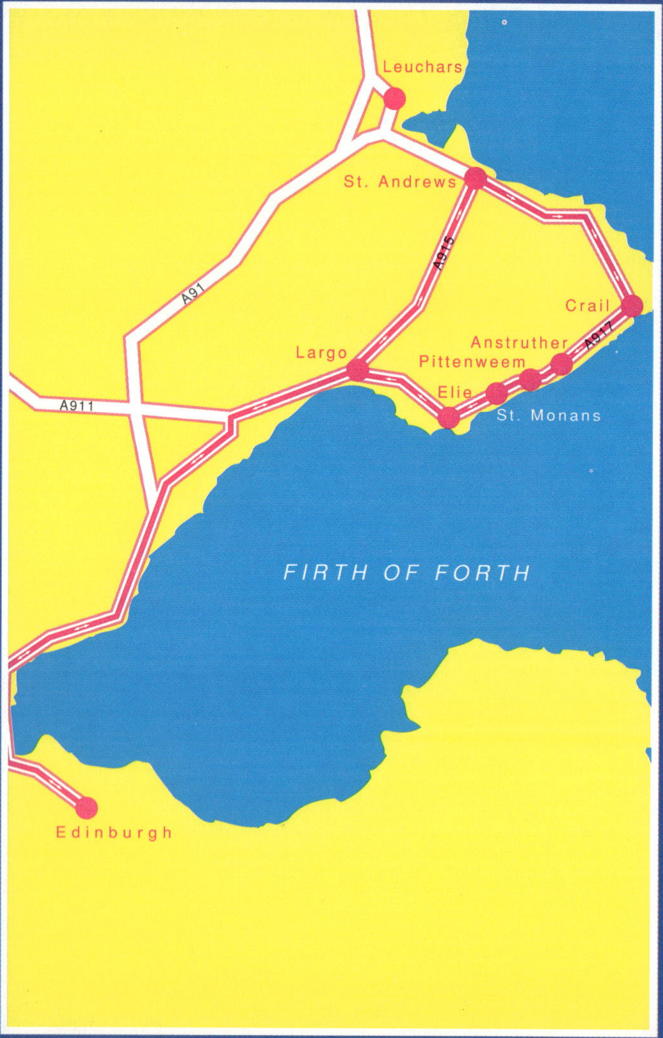
Leuchars
St. Andrews
A91
A915
Crail
Anstruther
A917
Largo
Pittenweem
Elie
St. Monans
A911
FIRTH OF FORTH
Edinburgh

## St. Andrews

*A one-day excursion to an historic, pretty seaside town.*

St. Andrews is 55 miles from Edinburgh on the M 90 and A 91, accessible by car or regular bus service. The nearest railway station is at Leuchars, about 4 miles away (trains from Waverley – see **Railways**). The city of St. Andrews is rich in historical associations. Founded by King David I in 1140, it became Scotland's ecclesiastical capital with the building of St. Andrews Cathedral. Begun in 1161, the cathedral flourished for four centuries until it was ransacked by the Reformers in 1599, after which it fell into ruin. The ruins are open to the public, and the 12thC St. Rule's Tower offers excellent views over the town. Nearby are the ruins of 13thC St. Andrews Castle with its sinister bottle-dungeon hewn out of the solid rock. The cathedral, castle and neighbouring museum are open 0930-1900 Mon.-Sat., 1400-1900 Sun. (close 1600 Oct.-Nov.). The museum also closes 1230-1330.

Pittenweem

St. Andrews also possesses Scotland's oldest university, dating from 1411, and lays claim to being the home of golf. The world-famous Old Course lies on the links to the north and is open to visitors. Other attractions include the Botanical Gardens, the fine sandy beaches and many pleasant coastal walks. The Tourist Information Centre is at 78 South St, St. Andrews, tel: 0334-72021.

From St. Andrews, return to Edinburgh by the A 917 and visit the picturesque fishing villages of the East Neuk of Fife. Crail has charming stone-built houses with distinctive pantile roofs and crow-stepped gables, the 12thC Church of St. Mary, a museum and an attractive harbour. Further on is Anstruther with the Scottish Fisheries Museum, the North Carr Lightship Museum and a restored 19thC fishing boat. There are boat trips to the Isle of May to see the seals and seabirds. The next village is Pittenweem, with its Flemish architecture and a daily market selling freshly-caught fish. St. Monans has a 14thC fishermen's church, the ruins of Newark Castle and a ruined windmill. Elie is an ideal spot for sailing, windsurfing and swimming, and Largo is the birthplace of Alexander Selkirk, the real-life castaway whose story provided the basis for *Robinson Crusoe*. There are Tourist Information Centres at Harbourhead, Anstruther, tel: 0333-310628, and the Museum, 11 Marketgate, Crail, tel: 0333-50869.

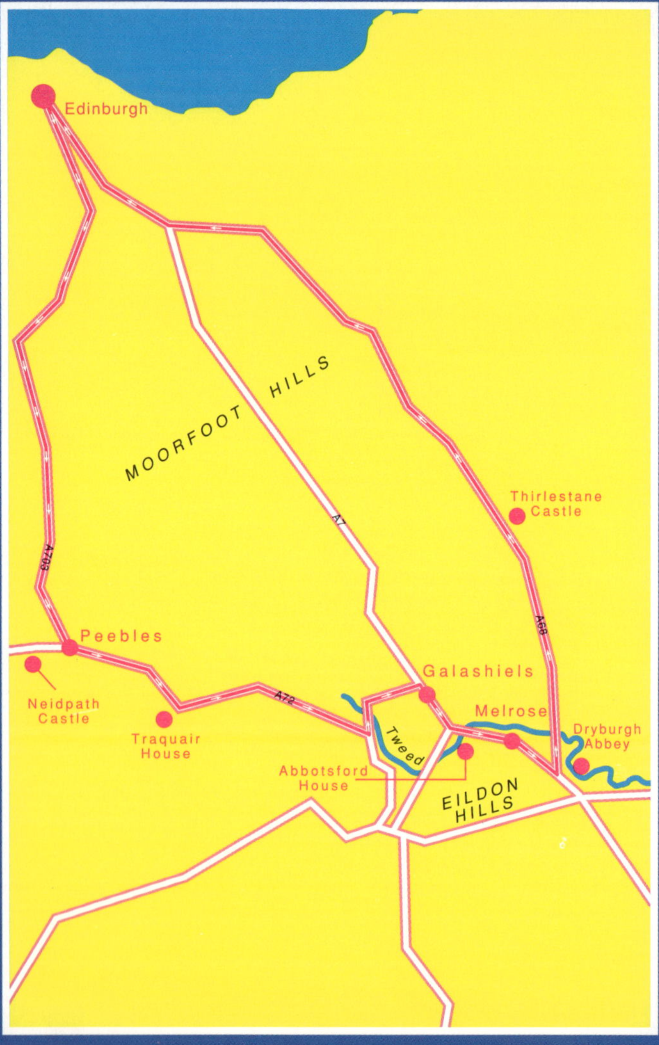
Edinburgh
MOORFOOT HILLS
A7
A703
A68
A72
Thirlestane Castle
Peebles
Galashiels
Melrose
Neidpath Castle
Traquair House
Tweed
Dryburgh Abbey
Abbotsford House
EILDON HILLS

# EXCURSION 2

## Scott Country

*A full-day excursion into the scenic Borders countryside. This area, to the south of Edinburgh, is historically associated with the life and work of Sir Walter Scott. Private transport is required.*

The Royal Burgh of Peebles (20 miles south of Edinburgh) is a picturesque little town situated on the River Tweed, with a local museum and the ruins of the 13thC Cross Kirk. There are beautiful walks along the river, especially to the west towards Neidpath Castle (1100-1700 Mon.-Sat., 1300-1700 Sun., Easter-Sep.; £1, child 50p).
Near Innerleithen is Traquair House (1330-1730 Easter & Spring Bank Holiday-Sep., 1030-1730 July & Aug.; £2.75, child £1.50), dating from the 12thC, which claims to be the oldest inhabited house in Scotland. You can admire its historic furniture, embroideries and books, and explore the cellars and secret stairways, or relax with a glass of Traquair Ale, brewed in the 18thC private brewhouse. There are also craft workshops and a tearoom and restaurant.
The next mill town is Galashiels, and nearby is Abbotsford House (1000-1700 Mon.-Sat., 1400-1700 Sun., mid Mar.-Oct.; £1.80, child 90p), the residence which Sir Walter Scott (see **A-Z**) built and lived in from 1812 until his death in 1832. See his study, his library with its rare books, the drawing room with hand-painted Chinese wallpapers, and his dining room overlooking the Tweed.
Beyond Melrose, situated at the foot of the Eildon hills with its fine 12thC Cistercian abbey, is the beautiful Dryburgh Abbey, founded in 1140. Sir Walter Scott is buried within the walls of the abbey. A mile from here, on the B 6356, is the famous 'Scott's View', a beauty spot overlooking the Tweed valley. Follow the A 68 for 49 miles back towards Edinburgh.
On the return journey stop to visit Thirlestane Castle, an ancient Border stronghold guarding the invasion route to the capital. Note especially the impressive stateroom with its ornate plaster ceiling and wood panelling, and the Border Country Life Exhibition, which displays aspects of life in the Borders from the earliest times onward. The castle and exhibition are open 1400-1700 Wed., Thu. & Sun. (Easter, May, June & Sep.), Sun.-Fri. (July & Aug.); the grounds are open 1200-1800; £3, child £2.50.

Abbotsford House

Blairgowrie
Dunkeld
Birnam
Tay
A9
A93
Scone
Palace
Perth
Tay
Kinross
Loch Leven
M90
FIRTH OF FORTH
Edinburgh

# Perth

*A one-day excursion to the 'Fair City'.*

Perth lies on the River Tay 42 miles north of Edinburgh and is accessible by car via the Forth Road Bridge (see **A-Z**) and the M 90 motorway, or by regular bus and train services.

En route from Edinburgh is Loch Leven, famed for the quality of its trout fishing, the gatherings of wildfowl and the historic Loch Leven Castle. The castle is an island fortress, accessible by boat from nearby Kinross. Mary, Queen of Scots, was held captive here in 1567.

The city of Perth is known variously as the Fair City, the Heart of Scotland and the Nation's Crossroads. At one time this was the lowest bridging point on the River Tay. You can visit St. Ninian's Cathedral, dating from 1849, with its magnificent stained-glass windows and beautiful rood screen, and the much older St. John's Kirk, founded in 1126. On the western edge of the city is the splendid 15thC Huntingtower Castle (0930-1900 Mon.-Sat., 1400-1900 Sun., April-Sep.; closes 1600 Oct.-Mar.; 60p, child 30p), whose fine architecture includes a remarkable painted ceiling. Other attractions in the town include Balhousie Castle with its Black Watch Regimental Museum, the Fair Maid's House, Branklyn Garden, and the Perth Museum and Art Gallery. And don't miss the chance of a walk on Kinnoul Hill, with lovely views over the Tay valley. The Tourist Information Centre is at The Round House, Marshall Pl., tel: 0738-38353.

Two miles out of town on the A 93 to Blairgowrie is the famous Scone Palace (0930-1700 Mon.-Sat., 0930-1330 Sun.; house and grounds £3.30, child £2; grounds only £1.65, child £1; family £10), where for 700 years the kings of Scotland were crowned. Collections on view include French furniture, china, ivories and Vernis Martin. There is an excellent restaurant and gift shop, and the extensive gardens and woods include a world-famous pinetum with the original Douglas fir.

Fourteen miles north of Perth on the A 9 are the attractive villages of Dunkeld and Birnam. Dunkeld was the ecclesiastical capital of Scotland in the 9thC, and has a cathedral and finely-preserved old houses in a picturesque riverside setting. There are also many pleasant walks in the surrounding woods, of which that at Birnam is famed in Shakespeare's *Macbeth*.

MONEY
FOR
PLANTS

TIONAL TRUST FOR SCOTLAND
KLYN GARDEN
N DAILY 10am – Sunset
ARCH – 31st OCTOBER
PLEASE
PUT MONEY
IN SLOT
SEED
WE HAVE SEED
OF MANY INTERESTING
SPECIES FOR SALE
IN THE HUT

Kinnoul Hill

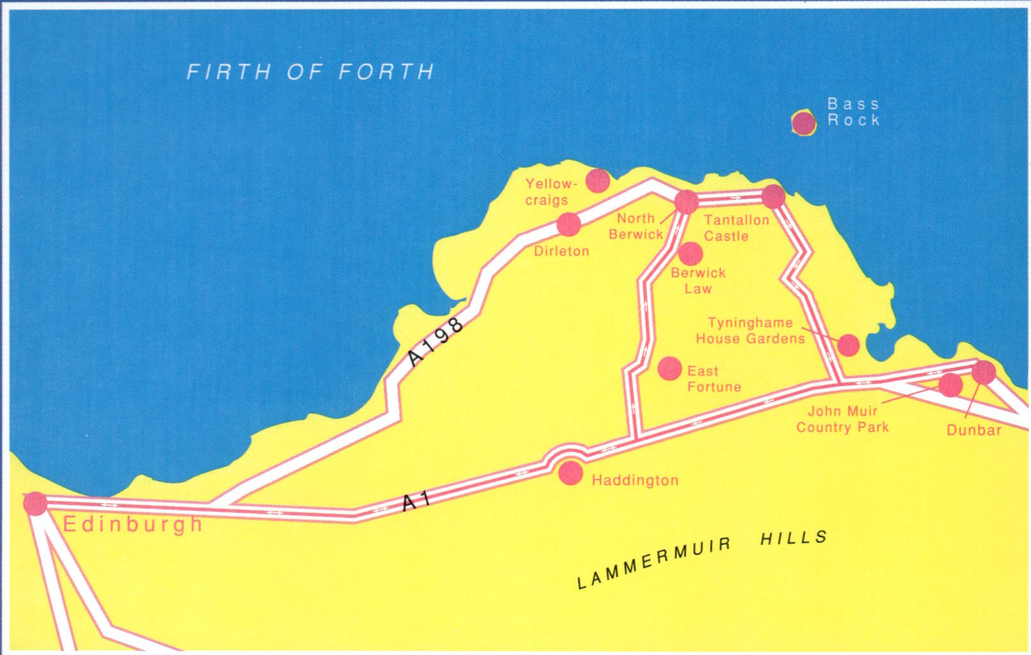
FIRTH OF FORTH
Bass Rock
Yellow-craigs
Dirleton
North Berwick
Tantallon Castle
Berwick Law
Tyninghame House Gardens
East Fortune
John Muir Country Park
Dunbar
A198
A1
Haddington
Edinburgh
LAMMERMUIR HILLS

# East Lothian

*A one- or two-day excursion exploring the lovely East Lothian coastline.*

East Lothian has many attractions for the visitor, including beaches, golf courses, nature trails and historic houses and castles. North Berwick and Dunbar are accessible by bus and train, Haddington by bus only. The Royal Burgh of Haddington, 18 miles east of Edinburgh, is an attractive market town with over 100 listed buildings of historic or architectural interest, including the 14thC Collegiate Church of St. Mary, the Town House, built by William Adam in 1748, with its distinctive spire, and Mitchell's Close, a 17thC tenement building restored in 1967, with many of its original features preserved. The Waterside Bistro, by the river, is a good spot for lunch.

North Berwick, north of Haddington on the B 1347, is a traditional seaside resort, overlooked by the prominent conical hill of Berwick Law (613 ft), visible from parts of Edinburgh on a clear day. There is a footpath to its summit, which bears a Napoleonic watchtower and a whalebone arch. Boat trips leave from the harbour to Bass Rock with its lighthouse and huge gannet colony (14,000 pairs of birds). The Tourist Information Centre is in Quality St, tel: 0620-2197.

A few miles to the west of North Berwick is the pleasant village of Dirleton, with its impressive 13thC castle, and access to the golden strand of Yellowcraigs beach, while to the south is the Museum of Flight at East Fortune. To the east of the town is the dramatic ruin of Tantallon Castle (0930-1900 Mon.-Sat., 1400-1900 Sun.; closes 1600 Oct.-Mar.), perched on a precarious cliff-top site.

Thirteen miles east along the coast is the pretty, twin-harboured fishing town of Dunbar, with the crumbling ruins of a 15thC castle dominating the harbour entrance. The town is the birthplace of John Muir (1838-1914), little known in Scotland but famed throughout America as the father of the nature conservation movement and founder of national parks. His childhood home in the High St is now a museum, and the John Muir Country Park to the west of the town provides cliff-top walks and nature trails. Nearby, Tyninghame House Gardens are open to the public in the summer months, offering colourful herbaceous borders and peaceful wooded and terraced gardens. There is a Tourist Information Centre at the Town House, High St, tel: 0368-63353.

BREADWINNER
SINCERITY II

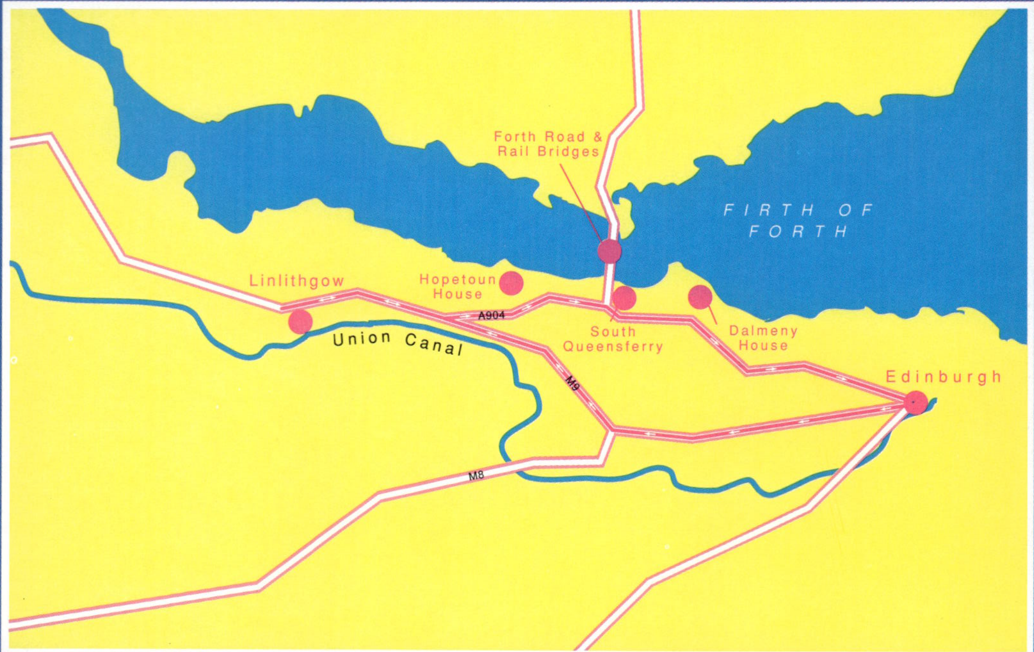
FIRTH OF
FORTH
Forth Road &
Rail Bridges
Linlithgow
Hopetoun
House
South
Queensferry
Dalmeny
House
Edinburgh
A904
Union Canal
M9
M8

# EXCURSION 5

## *Linlithgow*

*A half- or one-day excursion to this attractive and historic town.*

Linlithgow is 17 miles west of Edinburgh on the A 8 and M 9, and easily accessible by car, bus or train. Private transport is recommended for visiting Hopetoun and Dalmeny houses.

Linlithgow grew up around the 15th-17thC palace which still dominates the town, although today the structure is nothing more than a shell. It occupies a lovely setting on the shore of Linlithgow Loch. Mary, Queen of Scots, was born here in 1542. Nearby is the restored 15thC Church of St. Michael, with its controversial aluminium crown spire, added in 1964. The Union Canal passes through the town, and originally linked Edinburgh with the Forth & Clyde Canal at Falkirk. The canal was closed in the 1930s but is now being restored for the use of pleasure craft. Boat trips are available from Easter until Sep. There is a Canal Museum (1400-1700 Sat. & Sun., Easter-Sep.; free) at the basin, in the old stable that once housed the horses which were used to tow barges along the waterway. There are pleasant walks along the towpath, especially to the west to the spectacular Avon Aqueduct (built 1819-22), which carries the canal 86 ft above the River Avon.

North of the A 904 road from Linlithgow to South Queensferry lies the magnificent mansion of Hopetoun House (1000-1700 Easter & May-Sep.; £2.80, child £1.40), home of the Marquis of Linlithgow, and the finest Scottish example of the work of architect William Adam. Admire the sumptuous interiors, with priceless collections of paintings, china, tapestries, costumes and decorations, and stroll in the beautiful gardens overlooking the Firth of Forth (see **A-Z**).

On the far side of South Queensferry, beyond the Forth Road and Rail Bridges (see **A-Z**) is another stately home, Dalmeny House (1400-1730 Sun.-Thu., May-Sep.; £2.50, child £2), seat of the Earls of Rosebery. The present house dates from 1815 and was built in Tudor-Gothic style. The impressive art collection within includes 18thC French furniture, Goya tapestries and paintings by Gainsborough, Reynolds, Raeburn and Millais. The 5th earl was an authority on the life of Napoleon, and in addition to writing a book about the French emperor, collected many objects, paintings and pieces of furniture connected with him.

Hopetoun House

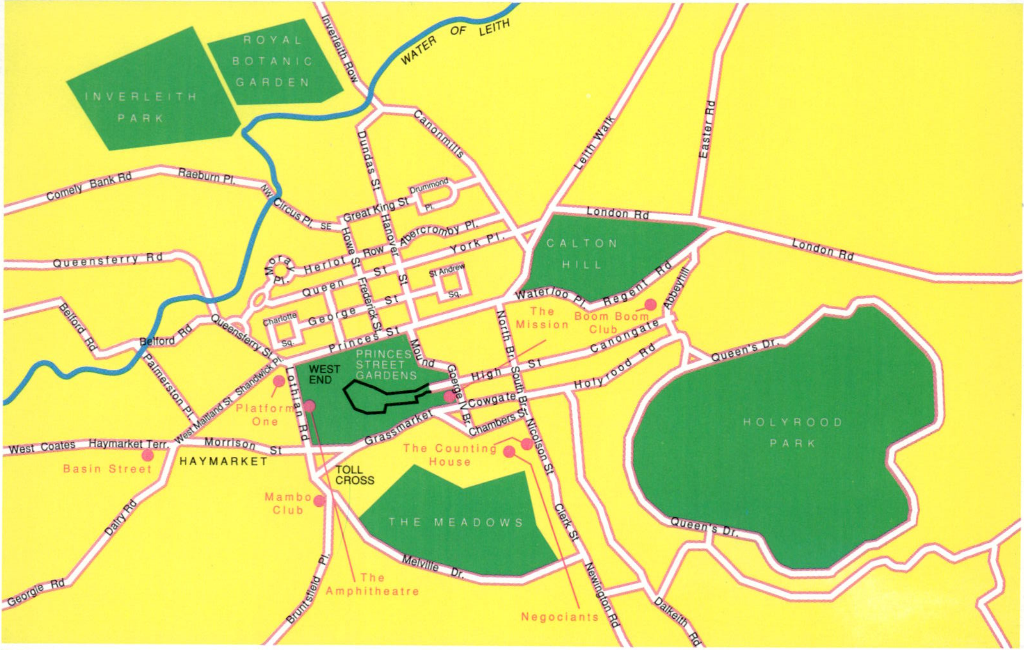
ROYAL BOTANIC GARDEN
INVERLEITH PARK
WATER OF LEITH
CALTON HILL
HOLYROOD PARK
PRINCES STREET GARDENS
THE MEADOWS
WEST END
HAYMARKET
TOLL CROSS
The Mission
Boom Boom Club
Platform One
The Counting House
Basin Street
Mambo Club
The Amphitheatre
Negociants
Inverleith Row
Canonmills
Leith Walk
Easter Rd
London Rd
Comely Bank Rd
Raeburn Pl.
NW Circus Pl. SE
Great King St
Drummond Pl.
Dundas St
Hanover St
Abercromby Pl.
York Pl.
Heriot Row
Howe St
Queensferry Rd
Moray Pl.
Queen St
St Andrew Sq.
George St
Frederick St
Charlotte Sq.
Princes St
Mound
Waterloo Pl.
Regent Rd
Abbeyhill
Belford Rd
Queensferry St
Canongate
North Br.
South Br.
High St
Holyrood Rd
Queen's Dr.
Goerge IV Br.
Cowgate
Chambers St
Nicolson St
Grassmarket
Lothian Rd
Shandwick Pl.
West Maitland St
Palmerston Pl.
West Coates
Haymarket Terr.
Morrison St
Dalry Rd
Georgie Rd
Bruntsfield Pl.
Melville Dr.
Clerk St
Newington Rd
Dalkeith Rd

**PLATFORM ONE** Rutland St.
■ Check listings for times and bands. ● Usually free.
*Comfortable bar which offers sessions of jazz, folk and R & B.*

**BASIN STREET** Haymarket Terr.
■ Check listings for times and bands. Bus 2, 3, 4, 12, 21, 22, 25, 26, 28, 29, 31, 33, 43, 44. ● Usually free.
*Pleasant pub with regular live jazz from local bands.*

**NEGOCIANTS** Bristo Sq., Teviot Row.
■ Check listings. Bus 2, 23, 24, 27. ● Free.
*A busy wine bar with live music downstairs on most nights.*

**THE AMPHITHEATRE** 31 Lothian Rd.
■ 2200-0400 Fri., 2330-0400 Sat., 2200-0300 Sun. Bus 9, 10, 11, 15, 16, 18, 34, 35, 62. ● £2-4, half price before 2300.
*The city's top nightclub. Over-21s only, no denim. Good laser show.*

**MAMBO CLUB** Network, 2-3 West Tollcross.
■ 2200-0300 Sat. Bus 9, 10, 11, 15, 16, 18, 34, 35, 62. ● £2.50.
*Lively and popular dance club with rhythms from around the world, especially African and calypso.*

**THE MISSION** Victoria St.
■ 2230-0300 Wed.-Sun. Bus 2, 12, 23, 24, 27, 40, 41, 42, 45, 46. ● £2.
*Two separate discos playing soul, hip-hop and funk.*

**BOOM BOOM CLUB** Calton Studios, Calton Rd.
■ 2200-0400 Sat. Bus 1, 6, 34, 35. ● £5.
*Plays the latest dance music and attracts a young and trendy crowd.*

**THE COUNTING HOUSE** 32-33 West Nicolson St.
■ Show begins 2200 Fri. & Sat. Bus 3, 7, 31, 33, 40, 41, 42, 46, 80, 81, 82, 87. ● £4.50.
*Café/bar venue for cabaret acts and stand-up comedy from all over Britain.*

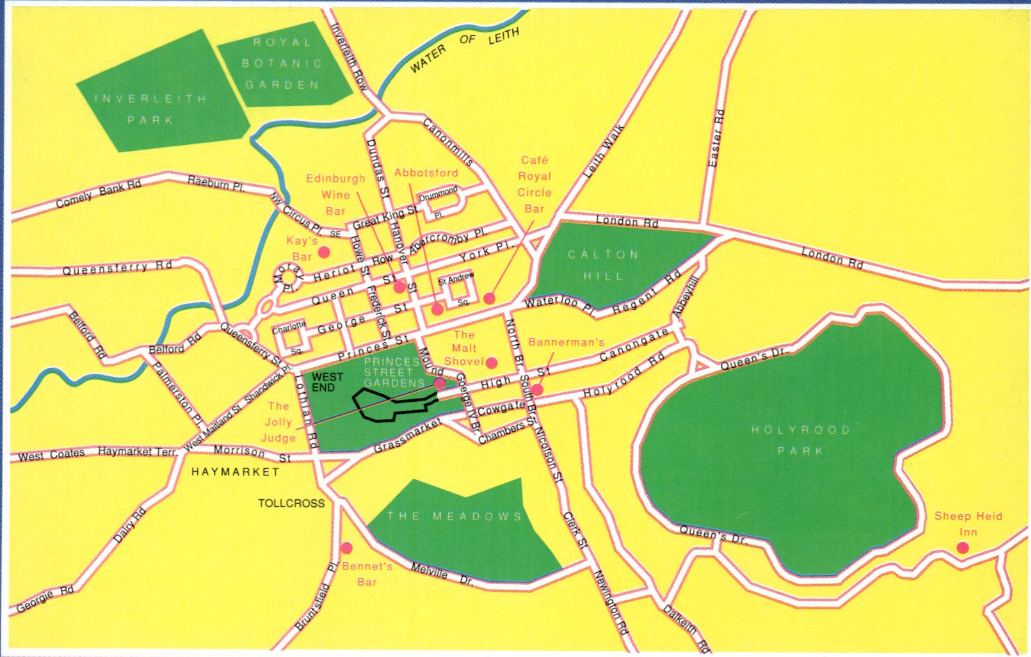

INVERLEITH PARK
ROYAL BOTANIC GARDEN
WATER OF LEITH
Inverleith Row
Canonmills
Comely Bank Rd
Raeburn Pl.
NW Circus Pl.
SE
Dundas St
Edinburgh Wine Bar
Abbotsford
Café Royal Circle Bar
Leith Walk
Easter Rd
London Rd
Drummond Pl.
Great King St
Hanover St
Abercromby Pl.
York Pl.
Kay's Bar
Queensferry Rd
Moray Pl.
Heriot Row
Howe St
Queen St
St Andrew Sq.
CALTON HILL
Waterloo Pl.
Regent Rd
Abbeyhill
George St
Frederick St
Charlotte Sq.
Belford Rd
Queensferry St
Princes St
The Malt Shovel
North Br.
Bannerman's
Canongate
PRINCES STREET GARDENS
WEST END
Mound
High St
South Br.
Holyrood Rd
Queen's Dr.
Shandwick Pl.
Palmerston Pl.
West Maitland St
Lothian Rd
The Jolly Judge
George IV Br.
Cowgate
Chambers St
Nicolson St
Grassmarket
HOLYROOD PARK
West Coates
Haymarket Terr.
Morrison St
HAYMARKET
TOLLCROSS
THE MEADOWS
Clerk St
Dalry Rd
Bennet's Bar
Bruntsfield Pl.
Melville Dr.
Newington Rd
Queen's Dr.
Sheep Heid Inn
Georgie Rd
Dalkeith Rd

**BENNET'S BAR** 8 Leven St.
Bus 9, 10, 11, 16, 23, 27, 45, 47.
*Beautiful Victorian interior with stained-glass windows and an ornamented ceiling. Food at lunchtime.*

**ABBOTSFORD** Rose St.
*Traditional pub with a richly carved 'island' bar and leather benches.*

**BANNERMAN'S** 55 Niddry St, Cowgate.
Bus 3, 5, 7, 21, 30, 31, 33, 87.
*Flagstone floors and barrel-vault ceiling. Attracts many students.*

**THE MALT SHOVEL** 13 Cockburn St.
*Comfortable lounge with a wide choice of beers and malt whiskies.*

**EDINBURGH WINE BAR** 110 Hanover St.
Bus 8, 9, 23, 27.
*Friendly and relaxed New Town (see* **A-Z***) watering hole.*

**SHEEP HEID INN** Causeway, Duddingston Village.
Bus 4, 42, 43, 44, 45, 46, 47.
*Delightful old-fashioned inn at the foot of Arthur's Seat (see* **A-Z***). There are a beer garden and skittles alley at the back.*

**THE JOLLY JUDGE** 7a James Court, Lawnmarket, Royal Mile.
Bus 23, 24, 27, 30, 34, 35, 40, 41, 42, 45, 46, 89.
*A small, snug, low-ceilinged hostelry in an Old Town (see* **A-Z***) close.*

**KAY'S BAR** 39 Jamaica St.
Bus 24, 28, 29, 41A.
*Former New Town (see* **A-Z***) wine merchant's shop converted into a cosy lounge, with classical music in the background.*

**CAFÉ ROYAL CIRCLE BAR** West Register St.
*Large, stylish Victorian pub, with a long oval bar in the middle, and attractive tile portraits of engineers and inventors on the walls.*

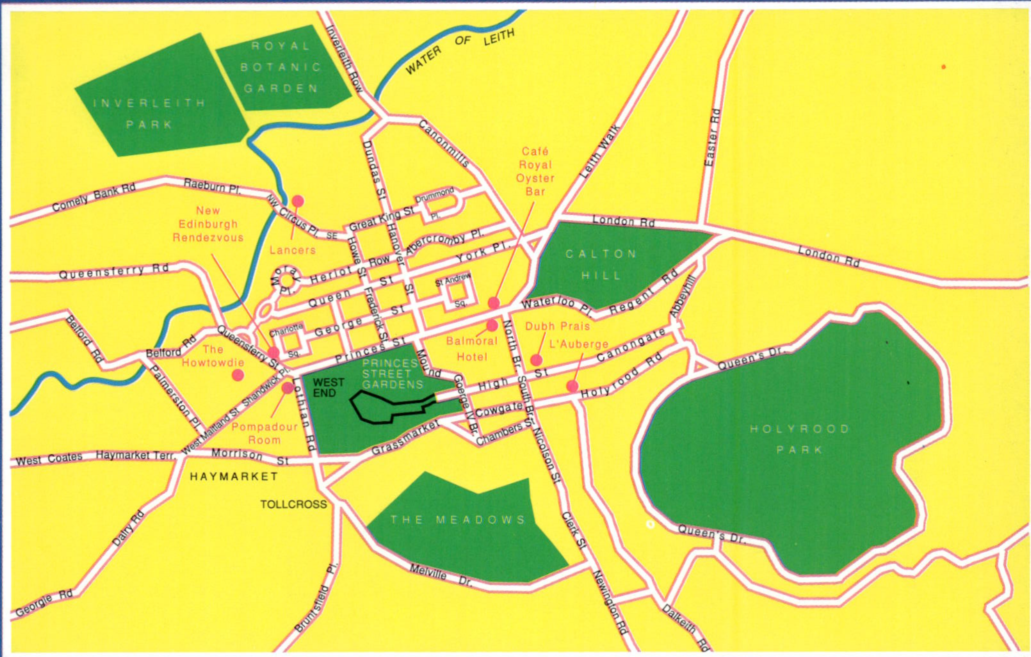
ROYAL BOTANIC GARDEN
INVERLEITH PARK
WATER OF LEITH
Inverleith Row
Canonmills
Café Royal Oyster Bar
Leith Walk
Easter Rd
Comely Bank Rd
Raeburn Pl.
NW Circus Pl. SE
New Edinburgh Rendezvous
Lancers
Dundas St
Drummond Pl.
Great King St
Abercromby Pl.
York Pl.
London Rd
CALTON HILL
Queensferry Rd
Moray Pl.
Heriot Row
Howe St
Hanover St
Queen St
St Andrew Sq.
Frederick St
George St
Charlotte Sq.
Waterloo Pl.
Regent Rd
Abbeyhill
Belford Rd
Queensferry St
The Howtowdie
Princes St
PRINCES STREET GARDENS
Mound
WEST END
Balmoral Hotel
North Br.
South Br.
Dubh Prais
L'Auberge
Canongate
Queen's Dr.
High St
Holyrood Rd
Shandwick Pl.
Lothian Rd
Palmerston Pl.
West Maitland St
Pompadour Room
Goerge IV Br.
Cowgate
Chambers St
Nicolson St
HOLYROOD PARK
Grassmarket
West Coates
Haymarket Terr.
Morrison St
HAYMARKET
TOLLCROSS
THE MEADOWS
Clerk St
Queen's Dr.
Dalry Rd
Melville Dr.
Newington Rd
Dalkeith Rd
Bruntsfield Pl.
Georgie Rd

**POMPADOUR ROOM** Caledonian Hotel, Princes St, tel: 2252433.
■ 1200-1400, 1930-2230 Mon.-Fri., 1930-2230 Sat. & Sun. ● Expensive.
*Traditional Scottish fare at lunch; international cuisine in the evenings.*

**THE HOWTOWDIE** 24a Stafford St, tel: 2256291.
■ 1200-1400, 1900-2300 Mon.-Fri., 1900-2300 Sat. Bus 2, 12, 26, 29, 31, 33, 85, 86. ● Expensive.
*Traditional Scottish cooking served in one of the city's best restaurants.*

**BALMORAL HOTEL** Princes St, tel: 5562414/5573777.
■ Daily. Bus 2, 12, 26, 29, 31, 33, 85, 86. ● Expensive.
*Reopened after a multimillion-pound facelift. Choose between the Grill Room with its huge open fire or the Continental-style Bridges Brasserie.*

**L'AUBERGE** 58 St. Mary's St, tel: 5565888.
■ 1215-1400, 1845-2130 Mon.-Sat., 1230-1400, 1845-2100 Sun. Bus 1, 6. ● Expensive.
*Genuine* nouvelle cuisine *can be enjoyed in this stylish restaurant.*

**CAFÉ ROYAL OYSTER BAR** 17a West Register St, tel: 5561884.
■ 1200-1400, 1900-2230. ● Expensive.
*The oldest seafood restaurant in Scotland. Interesting Victorian interior.*

**DUBH PRAIS** 123b High St, Royal Mile, tel: 5575732.
■ 1200-1500, 1800-2230 Mon.-Sat. Bus 3, 21, 30, 31, 33, 34, 35, 80, 81, 82. ● Moderate.
*Restaurant with relaxed atmosphere, specializing in fine Scottish cuisine.*

**NEW EDINBURGH RENDEZVOUS** 10a Queensferry St, tel: 2252023. ■ 1200-1400, 1730-2330 Mon.-Sat., 1300-2330 Sun. Bus 18, 19, 29, 34, 35, 40, 41, 80, 81, 85. ● Moderate.
*Sample some of the best Pekinese cuisine in Scotland.*

**LANCERS** 5 Hamilton Pl., Stockbridge, tel: 3323444/9559.
■ 1230-1430, 1730-2300. Bus 24, 29, 34. ● Moderate.
*A wide selection of excellent Bengali and northern Indian cuisine.*

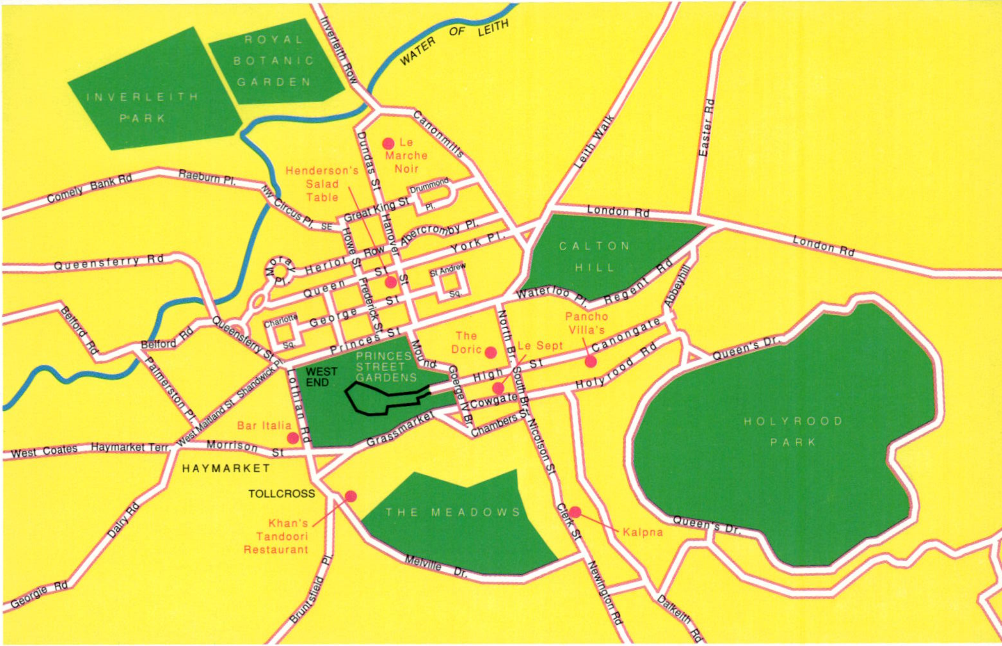

INVERLEITH PARK
ROYAL BOTANIC GARDEN
WATER OF LEITH
Inverleith Row
Canonmills
Le Marche Noir
Henderson's Salad Table
Dundas St
Comely Bank Rd
Raeburn Pl.
NW Circus Pl.
SE
Great King St
Drummond Pl.
Hanover St
Howe St
Abercromby Pl.
York Pl.
Row
Heriot Row
Queensferry Rd
Moray Pl.
Queen St
Frederick St
St Andrew Sq.
George St
Charlotte Sq.
Princes St
Belford Rd
Queensferry St
Palmerston Pl.
Shandwick Pl.
West Maitland St
West Coates
Haymarket Terr.
Morrison St
HAYMARKET
TOLLCROSS
Bar Italia
Lothian Rd
WEST END
PRINCES STREET GARDENS
Mound
Grassmarket
Khan's Tandoori Restaurant
Dalry Rd
Georgie Rd
Bruntsfield Pl.
Melville Dr.
THE MEADOWS
The Doric
Le Sept
George IV Br.
High St
Cowgate
Chambers St
North Br.
South Br.
Nicolson St
Clerk St
Newington Rd
Kalpna
Dalkeith Rd
Leith Walk
London Rd
CALTON HILL
Waterloo Pl.
Regent Rd
Abbeyhill
Easter Rd
Pancho Villa's
Canongate
Holyrood Rd
Queen's Dr.
HOLYROOD PARK

**LE MARCHE NOIR** 2-4 Eyre Pl., tel: 5581608.
■ 1200-1430, 1900-2230 Mon.-Sat. Bus 8, 19, 39, 23, 27. ● Moderate.
*Straightforward French country-style cooking.*

**PANCHO VILLA'S** 240 Canongate, Royal Mile, tel: 5574416.
■ 1200-1400, 1830-2230 Mon.-Fri., 1800-2300 Sat., 1900-2200 Sun. Bus 1, 6. ● Moderate.
*Informal atmosphere, delicious Mexican food. Live music on Sat. night.*

**HENDERSON'S SALAD TABLE** 94 Hanover St, tel: 2252131.
■ 0800-2300 Mon.-Sat. ● Moderate.
*Popular self-service restaurant offering a huge selection of salads.*

**LE SEPT** 7 Old Fishmarket Close, High St, Royal Mile, tel: 2255428.
■ 1200-1430, 1830-2230 Mon.-Sat., 1830-2230 Sun. Bus 23, 24, 27, 30, 34, 40, 41, 42, 45, 46, 89. ● Inexpensive-moderate.
*Classic French cuisine, with a less expensive brasserie upstairs.*

**KALPNA** 2-3 St. Patrick Sq., tel: 6679890.
■ 1200-1400, 1730-2330 Mon.-Sat. Bus 3, 7, 8, 21, 31, 33, 80, 82, 87.
● Inexpensive-moderate.
*A southern Indian, non-smoking, vegetarian restaurant.*

**THE DORIC** 15-16 Market St, tel: 2251084.
■ 1200-0100 Mon.-Wed., 1200-0200 Thu.-Sat., 1830-2300 Sun.
● Inexpensive-moderate.
*Bar and bistro serving a range of appetizing dishes.*

**KHAN'S TANDOORI RESTAURANT** 6 Brougham St, Tollcross, tel: 2291818/2285023. ■ 1700-0230. Bus 9, 10, 11, 15, 16, 18, 23, 24, 27. ● Inexpensive.
*Friendly curry house with generous helpings of traditional Indian dishes.*

**BAR ITALIA** 100 Lothian Rd, tel: 2286379/2290451.
■ 1700-0230. Bus 9, 10, 11, 15, 16, 18, 34, 35, 62. ● Inexpensive.
*Excellent pizzas and pasta dishes, ideal for hungry late-night revellers.*

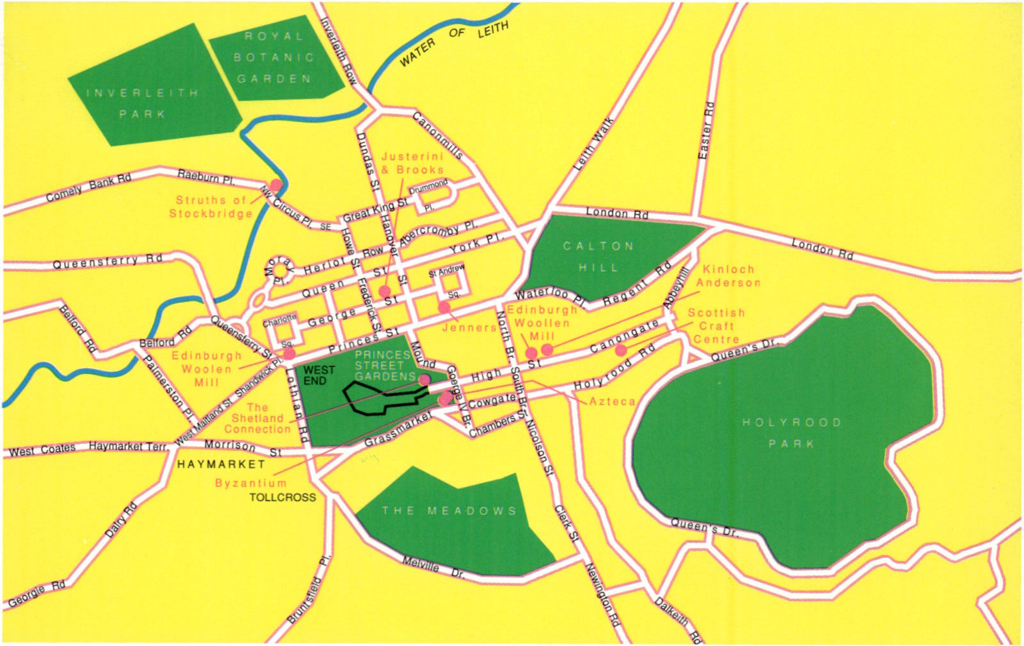

INVERLEITH PARK
ROYAL BOTANIC GARDEN
WATER OF LEITH
Inverleith Row
Canonmills
Leith Walk
Easter Rd
London Rd
Comely Bank Rd
Raeburn Pl.
Struths of Stockbridge
NW Circus Pl.
SE
Dundas St
Justerini & Brooks
Drummond Pl.
Great King St
Hanover St
Abercromby Pl.
York Pl.
Howe St
Row
Heriot
Queensferry Rd
Moray Pl.
Queen St
St Andrew Sq.
Frederick St
CALTON HILL
Regent Rd
Waterloo Pl.
Kinloch Anderson
Abbeyhill
Scottish Craft Centre
Canongate
Belford Rd
Charlotte Sq.
George St
Princes St
Jenners
North Br.
Edinburgh Woollen Mill
Queensferry St
Edinburgh Woolen Mill
Shandwick Pl.
WEST END
PRINCES STREET GARDENS
Mound
High St
Holyrood Rd
Queen's Dr.
George IV Br.
Cowgate
Azteca
South Br.
Chambers St
Nicolson St
Palmerston Pl.
The Shetland Connection
Lothian Rd
West Maitland St
Grassmarket
HOLYROOD PARK
West Coates
Haymarket Terr.
Morrison St
HAYMARKET
Byzantium
TOLLCROSS
THE MEADOWS
Clerk St
Queen's Dr.
Dalry Rd
Georgie Rd
Bruntsfield Pl.
Melville Dr.
Newington Rd
Dalkeith Rd

**JENNERS** Princes St, at the corner with South St. Andrew St.
■ 0900-1730 Mon.-Sat. (till 1930 on Thu.).
*Quality department store offering a huge selection of goods.*

**KINLOCH ANDERSON** 45 High St, Royal Mile.
■ 0900-1730 Mon.-Sat. (1700 Nov.-Mar.). Bus 3, 21, 31, 33, 34, 35, 80.
*The best in Highland dress, with a range of over 350 authentic tartans.*

**EDINBURGH WOOLLEN MILL** 139 Princes St & 51 High St.
■ 0900-1730 Mon.-Sat.
*Good value range of knitwear, tweeds, gloves, hats, bags and slippers.*

**THE SHETLAND CONNECTION** 491 Lawnmarket, Royal Mile.
■ 1000-2000 Sun.-Fri., 1000-2200 Sat. Bus 23, 24, 30, 35, 40, 46, 89.
*Handmade Shetland, Fair Isle and Aran knitwear in original designs.*

**BYZANTIUM** Victoria St.
■ 1000-1730 Mon.-Sat. Bus 23, 24, 27, 30, 40, 41, 42, 45, 46, 72, 89.
*A pleasant collection of shops selling antiques, paintings, jewellery, etc.*

**SCOTTISH CRAFT CENTRE** 140 Canongate, Royal Mile.
■ 1000-1730 Mon.-Sat. Bus 1, 6.
*Showcase for Scottish crafts, selling ceramics, pottery, textiles, jewellery.*

**AZTECA** 16 Victoria St.
■ 1000-1800 Mon.-Sat. (till 1900 during the Festival). Bus 23, 24, 27, 30, 40, 41, 42, 45, 46, 72, 89.
*Jewellery, tapestries and ceramics imported directly from South America.*

**JUSTERINI & BROOKS** 39 George St.
■ 0900-1800 Mon.-Fri.
*Over 130 brands of malt whisky, along with decanters, glasses, wines.*

**STRUTHS OF STOCKBRIDGE** 39 Deanhaugh St, Stockbridge.
■ 0900-1730 Mon.-Sat. Bus 24, 28, 29, 34, 35, 41.
*The finest haggis, prime Scottish beef and smoked salmon.*

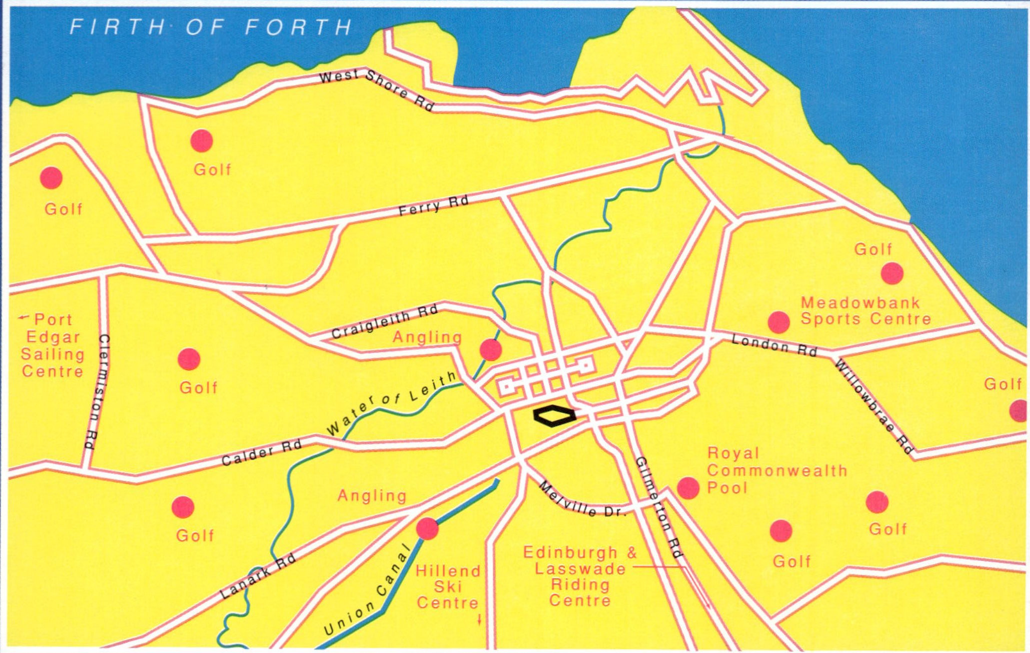
FIRTH OF FORTH
West Shore Rd
Golf
Golf
Ferry Rd
Golf
Meadowbank Sports Centre
← Port Edgar Sailing Centre
Clermiston Rd
Craigleith Rd
Angling
London Rd
Golf
Water of Leith
Willowbrae Rd
Golf
Calder Rd
Royal Commonwealth Pool
Angling
Melville Dr.
Gilmerton Rd
Golf
Golf
Golf
Lanark Rd
Union Canal
Hillend Ski Centre
Edinburgh & Lasswade Riding Centre

**MEADOWBANK SPORTS CENTRE** 139 London Rd.
■ 0900-2130. Bus 4, 5, 15, 26, 44. ● Cost based on facilities used.
*Sports centre and athletics stadium. Temporary membership is available. Facilities include fitness training, badminton, tennis, squash, cycling.*

**ROYAL COMMONWEALTH POOL** 21 Dalkeith Rd.
■ 0900-2100 Mon.-Fri., 1000-1600 Sat. & Sun. Bus 2, 12, 21, 33, 82, 83. ● £1 for pool, £1 for waterslides.
*The complex includes a 50 m main pool, 20 m learner's pool and a diving pool, as well as a multigym, sauna and waterslides.* See **CHILDREN**.

**GOLF** *Golf courses are plentiful – there are 28 within the city limits and over 80 within 20 miles of the city centre. Most clubs welcome visitors. For details, contact the Tourist Information Centre in Waverley Market.*

**ANGLING** *The waters around Edinburgh are well stocked with brown and rainbow trout (trout season: April-Sep.), and there is fishing for pike, perch and roach on the Union Canal. Contact the Tourist Centre. The booklet* Guide to Freshwater Fishing in the Lothian Region *is available free from the Dept of Planning, Lothian Region Council, 12 St. Giles St.*

**PORT EDGAR SAILING CENTRE** South Queensferry (10 miles west of the city). ■ 1000-2100 Easter-Oct. Bus: Eastern Scottish from St. Andrew Sq. bus station. ● 2 hr sessions: sailboard £5.30; Topper dinghy £6.10; Wayfarer dinghy £16.
*Sailboards and sailing dinghys for hire.*

**EDINBURGH & LASSWADE RIDING CENTRE** Kevock Rd, Lasswade. Bus 80, 84. ● £8 per hr, inc. hire of hard hat.
*Organized pony-trekking through the countryside around Edinburgh.*

**HILLEND SKI CENTRE** Biggar Rd, Fairmilehead.
■ 0930-2200 Sep.-April; 0930-2100 Mon.-Fri. (Sat. & Sun. 1700) May-Aug. Bus 4, 62. ● 1 hr, inc. equipment: Mon.-Fri. £3.25, Sat. & Sun. £3.95.
*The longest artificial ski-slope in Britain. There is a chair lift and tows, and the slope is floodlit at night. There's also a cafeteria with a bar.*

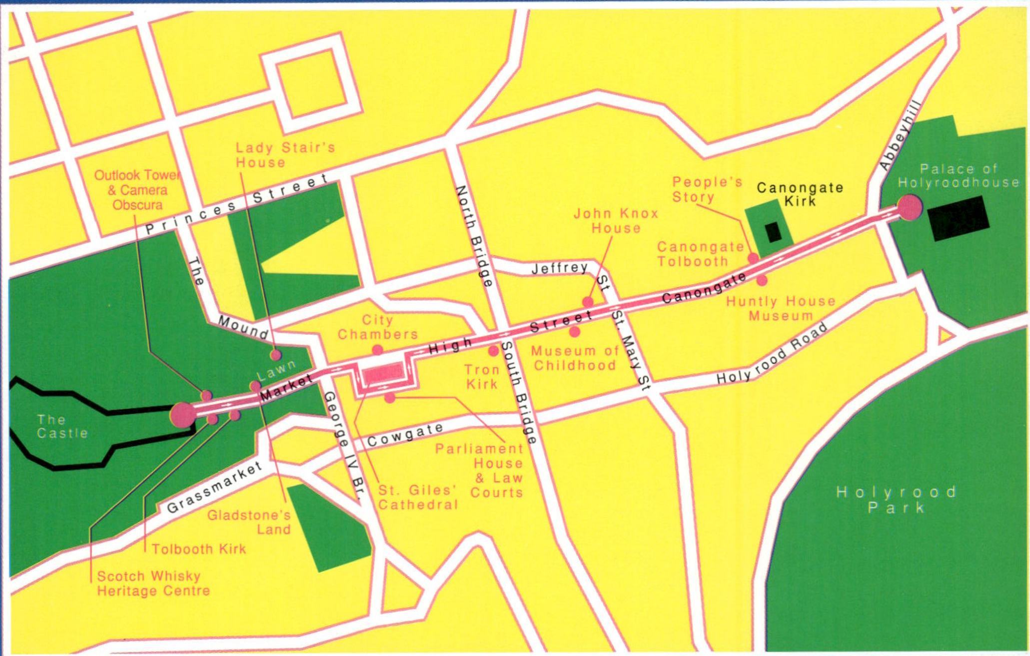

Lady Stair's House
Outlook Tower & Camera Obscura
Princes Street
The Mound
North Bridge
Jeffrey St
John Knox House
People's Story
Canongate Kirk
Palace of Holyroodhouse
Abbeyhill
Canongate Tolbooth
Canongate
Huntly House Museum
St. Mary St
Holyrood Road
High Street
Museum of Childhood
City Chambers
Tron Kirk
South Bridge
Lawn Market
The Castle
George IV Br.
Cowgate
Parliament House & Law Courts
St. Giles' Cathedral
Grassmarket
Gladstone's Land
Tolbooth Kirk
Scotch Whisky Heritage Centre
Holyrood Park

## The Royal Mile

Duration: 2-4 hr.

This historic thoroughfare (see **Royal Mile**) links two of the city's main tourist attractions, the Castle (see **EDINBURGH CASTLE**, **A-Z**) and the Palace of Holyroodhouse (see **A-Z**). There is much to see and the time required will depend on how many stops you make to visit the various museums and buildings.

Begin at the Castle Esplanade. On the right is 'Cannonball House' (built 1630). The cannonball lodged in the wall was not fired in anger, but marks the gravitation height of the city's first piped water supply. Across the street is a fountain (dated 1722) which marks the spot where hundreds of women were burnt as witches. At the corner with Ramsay Lane is the Outlook Tower & Camera Obscura (see **CHILDREN**), while on the right is the Scotch Whisky Heritage Centre (see **A-Z**). As you descend Castlehill, the Tolbooth Kirk (1842-44) comes into view; its 240 ft spire is the tallest in Edinburgh.

A few yards beyond the kirk, on the left, is Gladstone's Land (see **A-Z**), and through the close you will find Lady Stair's House (see **A-Z**). Cross George IV Bridge (a brass plaque in the road on the right-hand side marks the site of the city's last public execution in 1864), and go right into Parliament Sq. Brass plaques in the cobblestones in front of St. Giles' Cathedral (see **A-Z**) mark the outline of the Tolbooth (old town gaol, demolished in 1817), while the Heart of Midlothian (see **A-Z**) marks the site of the condemned cell. After visiting the Parliament House and Law Courts (see **A-Z**), leave the square at the Mercat Cross, opposite the splendid City Chambers (John Adam, 1761). At the downhill end of the chambers is Anchor Close, where in 1768 William Smellie printed the first edition of the *Encyclopaedia Britannica*. On the junction with South Bridge stands the Tron Kirk, which dates from 1637 (named after the tron, or weighing machine, that once stood here). Continue over South Bridge, and on the left is Paisley Close, with an inscription above the entrance which reads *Heave awa' chaps, I'm no' deid yet,* the words of a man who was rescued from a tenement collapse here in 1861. Downhill on the right is the Museum of Childhood (see **CHILDREN**), and where the street narrows is the distinctive John Knox House (see **A-Z**). At the junction with St. Mary's St and Jeffrey St more brass plaques mark the outline of the Netherbow Port (built 1513,

Canongate Tolbooth

demolished 1764), one of six gates in the old wall. Its original appearance can be seen in a display in Huntly House Museum (see below). Continue down the Canongate, passing on the right Chessel's Court, where Deacon Brodie (see **A-Z**) was caught robbing the Excise Office and was subsequently hanged. Further down is Huntly House Museum (see **ART GALLERIES & MUSEUMS**), and across the street, the Canongate Tolbooth (see **A-Z**) and the People's Story (see **CHILDREN**) museum. Next to the Tolbooth is Canongate Kirk (1688). The kirkyard contains the graves of Adam Smith, the economist, and the poet Robert Fergusson. Fergusson's headstone was erected by Robert Burns (see **A-Z**) and later renovated by R. L. Stevenson (see **A-Z**). Near the foot of the Canongate, on the left, is White Horse Close, a converted 17thC coaching inn which was the departure point for the stagecoach to London.
Cross the roundabout to Abbey Strand and finish your walk at the gates to Holyroodhouse, which were erected in 1922 as part of a memorial to King Edward VII.

Evening News
LLS YOU SIX
AYS A WEEK
CALEDONIAN SECURITY SERVICES
EBOOKSMAPS
Newsweek
363
Royal M
WE BUY ANTIQUE SILVER.
la casa
ANTIQ

1875
Curios
363
361
WE BUY
ANTIQUE
JEWELLERY

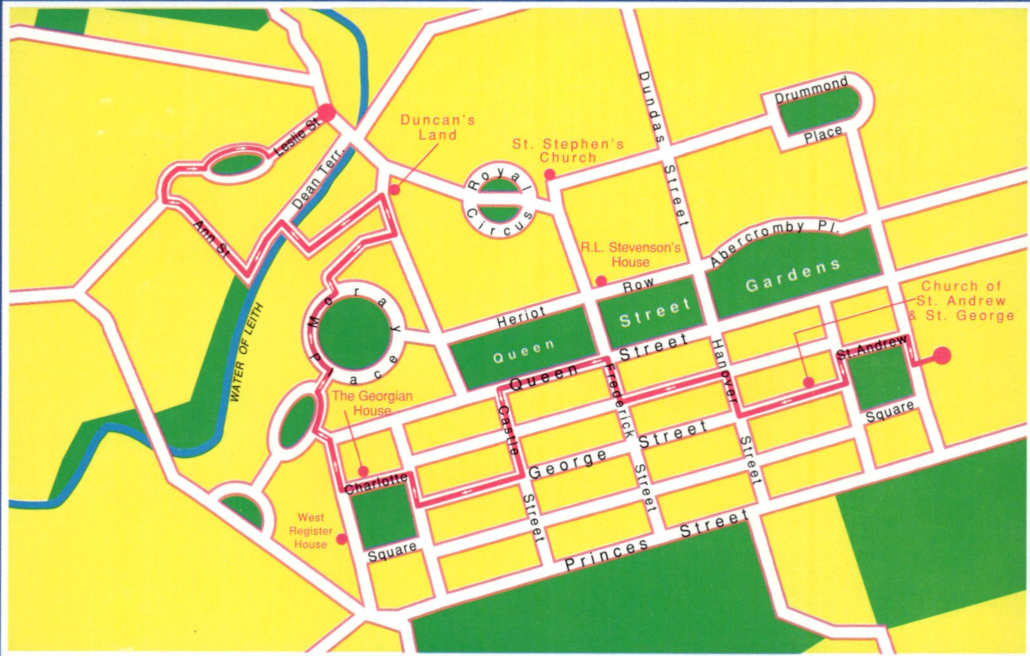
Leslie St.
Dean Terr.
Ann St
WATER OF LEITH
Duncan's Land
St. Stephen's Church
Royal Circus
Dundas Street
Drummond Place
Abercromby Pl.
R.L. Stevenson's House
Heriot Row
Gardens
Queen Street
Moray Place
The Georgian House
Charlotte Square
West Register House
Castle Street
Frederick Street
Hanover Street
George Street
Princes Street
Church of St. Andrew & St. George
St. Andrew Square

## The New Town

Duration: 1.5-2 hr.
Begin in St. Andrew Sq., in front of the Royal Bank of Scotland building built in 1772-74 as a house for Sir Lawrence Dundas. Go around the north side, which has some of the New Town's (see **A-Z**) earliest houses, and go along George St. On the right is the Church of St. Andrew and St. George (1782), with an interesting oval interior. Go right into Hanover St then left along Thistle St. This and Rose St were built to house the humbler folk of the New Town. Today Thistle St is lined with bistros, cafés and antique shops. Turn right down Frederick St, with a view of St. Stephen's Church (William Playfair, 1828), one of the New Town's most distinctive landmarks. Turn left into Queen St, with its private gardens (1823). The lake and island in these gardens are said to have been the inspiration for R. L. Stevenson's *Treasure Island*; the author (see **A-Z**) lived in Heriot Row, across the gardens. Turn left up North Castle St; No. 39 was the home of Sir Walter Scott (see **A-Z**) from 1802-26. Turn right into George St and right again to Charlotte Sq., going around the north side, whose magnificent façade was designed by Robert Adam, with modifications by Robert Reid. It was built in 1792-1805. At No. 5 is the headquarters of the National Trust for Scotland, No. 6 houses the office of the Secretary of State for Scotland and No. 7 the restored Georgian House (see **ART GALLERIES & MUSEUMS**). The dome on the west side belongs to West Register House, originally St. George's Church. Alexander Graham Bell, inventor of the telephone, lived at the corner of the square and South Charlotte St.
Leave the square by Glenfinlas St. Ainslie Pl., along with Randolph Cres. and Moray Pl., forms the Moray Estate, an impressive development built 1822-27. Go through Great Stuart St and round Moray Pl., turning left at Doune Terr. (with views of Stockbridge and Fettes College), and left again down Gloucester St to Duncan's Land, built as a house about 1746 (the lintel dated 1605 was brought from a house in the Old Town) but which is now a restaurant. From here go left into India Pl., right over the Water of Leith (see **WALK 4**), then left up Dean Terr. and right into Ann St, one of the prettiest streets in the city, built 1816-27 for Sir Henry Raeburn and named after his wife. At the end of the street go right into Dean Park Cres. and on to St. Bernard's Cres. Walk left into Leslie Pl. to finish in Stockbridge (see **CITY DISTRICTS**).

17

PITT
BANK OF SCOTLAND

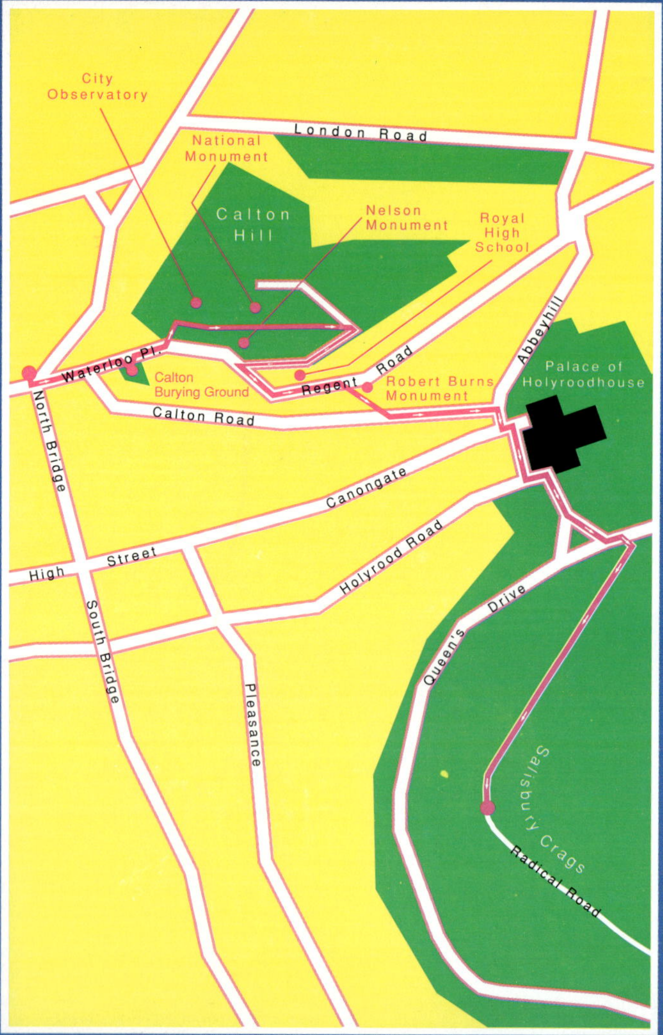
City Observatory
London Road
National Monument
Calton Hill
Nelson Monument
Royal High School
Waterloo Pl.
Calton Burying Ground
Regent Road
Robert Burns Monument
Abbeyhill
Palace of Holyroodhouse
Calton Road
North Bridge
Canongate
Holyrood Road
High Street
South Bridge
Queen's Drive
Pleasance
Salisbury Crags
Radical Road

## Calton Hill

Duration: 2-3 hr.
Begin at the east end of Princes St (see **A-Z**), in front of the impressive Register House, designed by Robert Adam and built 1774-88. This is the place where those hoping to trace their Scots ancestry begin their search. Head into Waterloo Pl. and cross Waterloo Bridge with its memorial arches and dramatic views. On the right is the Calton Burying Ground with its obelisk commemorating Australia's political martyrs of 1793 and the graves of many of Edinburgh's prominent citizens. Cross the street to a flight of stairs; climb up these then turn right up a path to the top of Calton Hill (see **A-Z**).
The summit of Calton Hill bristles with monuments and helped to earn Edinburgh the title 'Athens of the North'. The most impressive is the unfinished National Monument, with its twelve columns. It was begun in the early 1820s as a memorial to the dead of the Napoleonic Wars, but funds ran out and it was never completed. The 100 ft-high Nelson Monument (built 1807) is today used as a private residence, but you can climb the steps to the top for superb views (1300-1800 Mon., 1000-1800 Tue.-Sat., April-Sep.; 1000-1500 Mon.-Sat., Nov.-Mar.; 60p). Nearby are Dugald Stewart's Monument (1831) and the City Observatory (1818), both designed by William Playfair. Descend by the path beyond the Nelson Monument and exit onto Regent Rd. To the right is St. Andrew's House (government offices). Cross the road to enjoy views over the Old Town (see **A-Z**) and Arthur's Seat (see **A-Z**), then head left along Regent Rd. On the left above the road is the Greek Doric edifice of the former Royal High School (built 1825-29) and on the right is a monument to Robert Burns (see **A-Z**), built in 1830. Retrace your steps for a few yards and go through the gate on the left and descend the path leading down to Calton Rd. Walk left along this road to reach the foot of the Royal Mile (see **WALK 1**, **A-Z**).
The last part of this walk is for those still feeling energetic, and good walking shoes are recommended. Go along Horse Wynd and turn left into Holyrood Park. Salisbury Crags tower above. Where the rocks end there is a flight of stairs: climb these, then turn right and climb up the steep track. This path goes all the way along the foot of the crags and is known as the Radical Road. The views from here are superb, looking over the Old Town and the Firth of Forth (see **A-Z**) to the county of Fife.

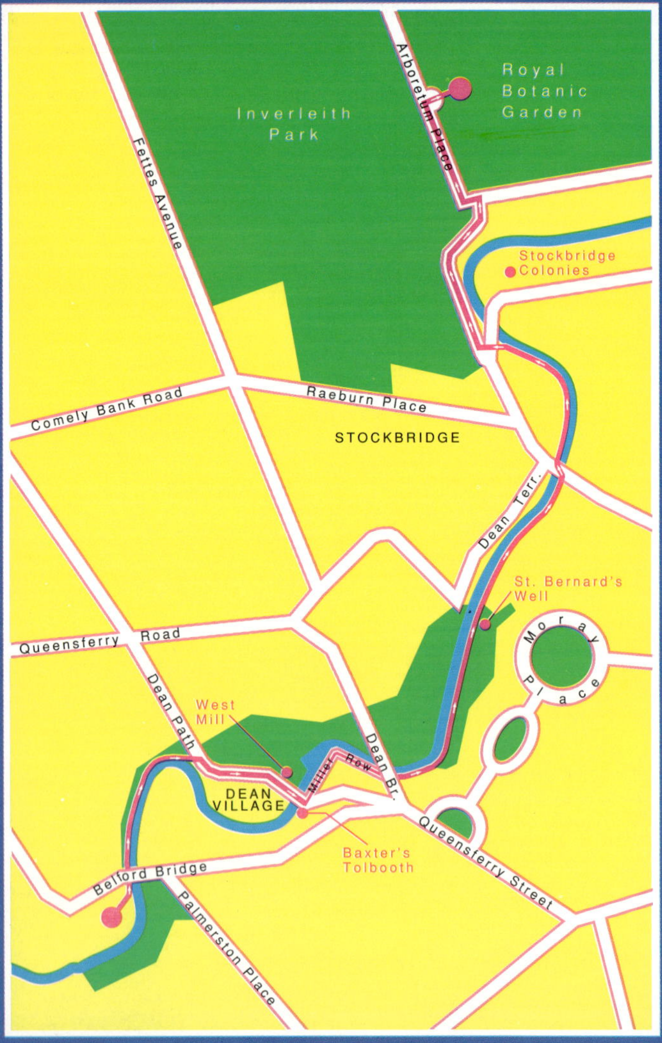
Royal
Botanic
Garden
Arboretum Place
Inverleith
Park
Fettes Avenue
Stockbridge
Colonies
Comely Bank Road
Raeburn Place
STOCKBRIDGE
Dean Terr.
St. Bernard's
Well
Moray
Place
Queensferry
Road
Dean Path
West
Mill
Miller
Row
Dean Br.
DEAN
VILLAGE
Baxter's
Tolbooth
Queensferry Street
Belford Bridge
Palmerston Place

# Water of Leith

Duration: 1 hr.

Begin at the Hilton National Hotel, Belford Rd (bus: LRT 41 to Dean Bridge, then walk along Belford Rd; Eastern Scottish C13 to the hotel). Go down the road named Bells Mills to reach the walkway on the bank of the river. The Water of Leith rises in the Pentland Hills (see **A-Z**) and flows 23 miles to the sea at Leith, its deep, wooded valley cutting a leafy swathe through the city. Go left, passing under Belford Bridge (built 1885-87). Beyond the bridge the path passes through the woods then descends beside a weir to a footbridge in the picturesque Dean Village (see **CITY DISTRICTS**). The Incorporation of Baxters (Baker's Union) once managed 11 mills and two granaries here. Cross the footbridge and go left along the far bank, then up narrow, cobbled Hawthornbank Lane to reach Bell's Bridge. On your left is Baxter's Tolbooth. A carved stone over the door shows baker's shovels with three loaves, and the words 'GOD BLESS THE BAXTERS OF EDIN BRUGH UHO BULT THIS HOUS 1675' [sic]. Across the road on the parapet of the bridge are more carved stones, and on the far side of the river is the huge West Mill, rebuilt in 1805 and now converted into flats. It is the largest surviving industrial building of that era. The steep hill leading up from the bridge, Bells Brae, was once the main road out of Edinburgh, heading to Queensferry. Go left down Miller Row. On the left beside the weir is the site of Lindsay's Mill, of which three millstones remain as a monument in the little park beyond. Continue under the 106 ft arches of Dean Bridge, built by Thomas Telford in 1832. The path now passes beneath Moray Bank Pl. Gardens (private) to reach St. Bernard's Well (1789). This was once a mineral spring; the statue is of Hygeia, goddess of health. Go down the stairs at the well and follow the riverside path under St. Bernard's Bridge to Stockbridge. Cross the bridge to the left and descend the stairs on the far side to the continuation of the walkway and follow this to Falshaw Bridge. Bear left across the road and go right into Arboretum Ave. On the left are playing fields, with the Gothic spires of Fettes College beyond. The neat terraced houses across the river to the right are the Stockbridge Colonies, a 19thC development built by an artisan's cooperative to provide affordable housing for tradesmen. Walk along Arboretum Pl. to end your walk at the entrance to the Royal Botanic Garden (see **A-Z**).

Stockbridge Colonies

ΘΕΟΣ
DEVS
GOD

OLIVER & BOYD

**Arthur's Seat:** A familiar Edinburgh landmark, this craggy hill rises above Holyroodhouse (see **A-Z**) to a height of 823 ft. A walk to its summit will be rewarded with panoramic views over the city. It was named in the 15thC during a revival of interest in Arthurian romances.

Arthur's Seat

**Burke & Hare:** William Burke and William Hare were notorious murderers who once prowled the streets and closes of Edinburgh's Old Town (see **A-Z**). In 1827 they strangled at least 16 people and sold the corpses to surgeons for medical research. Hare finally confessed to the horrific crimes and testified against Burke in a sensational trial. Burke was hanged in the Grassmarket (see **A-Z**) on 28 Jan. 1829, and his own corpse was subsequently dissected. His skeleton remains to this day in Edinburgh University's Department of Anatomy.

Burns Monument

**Burns, Robert (1759-96):** The poet Robert Burns is known and loved the world over through such classics as *Tam o'Shanter, My Love is like a Red, Red Rose* and *Auld Lang Syne*. Born in Alloway in Ayrshire, Burns first came to Edinburgh in 1768 to make his name in the Scottish capital, which he did – the Edinburgh edition of his poems sold 3000 copies. On a later visit he fell in love with Mrs Agnes Maclehose (the 'Clarinda' of his poems), who inspired the moving love-song, *Ae Fond Kiss*. She is buried in Canongate Kirkyard. His last visit to the city was in 1791, when he lodged at the White Hart Inn in the Grassmarket (see **A-Z**). There is a monument to Burns on Regent Rd (see **WALK 3**), and relics associated with him are in Lady Stair's House (see **A-Z**).

**Calton Hill:** This is the rocky hill rising to 328 ft at the east end of Princes St (see **A-Z**). Its summit is crowned with a number of interesting monuments. See **WALK 3.**

**Canongate Tolbooth:** This 16thC building with its prominent clock lies towards the foot of the Royal Mile (see **A-Z**) and was once the town hall and courtroom for the burgh of Canongate, which lay outside the Edinburgh city walls. It now houses the People's Story museum. See **CHILDREN**, **WALK 1**.

**Charlotte Square:** See WALK 2.

**Deacon Brodie:** Eighteenth-century city councillor Deacon William Brodie was, by day, a well-respected businessman. But at night he lived a secret life as a gambler, rogue and burglar, stealing to support his gambling debts, two mistresses and five illegitimate children. He was finally caught in the act of robbing the Excise Office in Chessel's Court, Canongate (see WALK 1), and was hanged at the Tolbooth on 1 Oct. 1788, in front of a crowd of 40,000. His double life is said to have been the inspiration behind R. L. Stevenson's (see **A-Z**) story of *Dr Jekyll and Mr Hyde.*

**Edinburgh Castle:** Perched on its volcanic crag, Edinburgh's castle dominates the city below. There has been a fortification on the Castle Rock since at least the 6thC, but the first proper fortress and royal resi-

Edinburgh Castle

dence were built in the 11thC for Malcolm Canmore and his Saxon queen, Margaret. Her son, David I, is thought to have built St. Margaret's Chapel, the oldest surviving building on the rock (and in the city), when he moved the Scottish capital from Dunfermline to Edinburgh in 1124. Since that time the castle has been added to gradually, attaining its present form around the beginning of the 20thC. The castle's last active role in military conflict was in 1745, during the Jacobite uprising. Today its military links remain strong: it is the Regimental Headquarters of the Royal Scots and Royal Scots Dragoon Guards, the home of the Army School of Piping and the setting for the famous annual Military Tattoo (see **A-Z**). See **EDINBURGH CASTLE, WALK 1**.

**Edinburgh Crystal Visitor Centre:** Eastfield, Penicuik, Midlothian (25 miles south of the city), tel: 0968-75128/72244. Here you can watch the production of fine crystal glassware, including glass-blowing, cooling, cutting, polishing and engraving. Guided tours of the works are available 0915-1530 Mon.-Fri.; £1, child 10-16 years 50p (for safety reasons, no children under 10 are allowed on the tours). There is also a large factory shop selling glassware and tableware, which is open 0900-1700 Mon.-Sat. (1000-1700 Sun., April-Sep.) but closed 25 Dec.-6 Jan.

**Edinburgh International Festival:** The world's largest arts festival is held for three weeks every Aug. and the city's population doubles as over 500,000 visitors and performers arrive. From its beginnings in 1947 the festival has grown and produced many offshoots, notably the Festival Fringe (see **A-Z**) and the Jazz, Film and Book festivals. The Military Tattoo (see **A-Z**), although not part of the main festival, is held at the same time. For information send postal enquiries to the Edinburgh Festival Society, 21 Market St, Edinburgh EH1 1BW, tel: 2264001. You can get information on the Film Festival from the Edinburgh Filmhouse, 88 Lothian Rd, Edinburgh, tel: 2284051. The Book Festival takes place every two years (on odd-numbered years) and programmes are available from the Scottish Book Centre, 137 Dundee St, Edinburgh EH11 1BG, tel: 2285444.

**Edinburgh Zoo:** Founded in 1913, the zoo occupies a pleasant 30 hectare site on Corstorphine Hill. It has over 2000 animals, including pygmy hippos, gorillas, snowy owls and a pair of rare snow leopards. It is famous for its colony of penguins, which go on a 'Penguin Parade' at 1430 daily, April-Sep. Another popular attraction is sea lion feeding time at 1500 daily. Facilities include a children's farm, adventure playground, restaurant, bookshop and picnic areas. There are also magnificent views from the top of the hill. See CHILDREN.

**Festival Fringe:** This famous offshoot of the Edinburgh International Festival (see **A-Z**) had its origins in eight small theatre companies that were excluded from the first official Festival in 1947. They went ahead and staged their productions anyway, and began a tradition which has blossomed into an annual extravaganza of nearly 1000 shows in 130 venues, selling 470,000 tickets. None of the performers are invited – they simply apply for a venue, turn up and do their own thing. The Fringe offers something for everyone, from theatre, comedy, cabaret and revue, to mime, dance, classical music, exhibitions, children's shows, opera, jazz, poetry, performance art, rock music and street entertainment. For information send postal enquiries to The Fringe Office, 180 High St, Edinburgh EH1 1QS, tel: 2265257. Programmes and ticket order forms are usually available from early July onward. During the Fringe, an Information Desk is to be found in the Fringe Office on the Royal Mile, open 1000-1800 daily. The Fringe Daily Diary, a free list of all Fringe events taking place on any day, is available from tourist centres, hotels, venues, etc.

**Firth of Forth:** The name for the estuary of the River Forth, the long, narrow arm of the sea that cuts into the Scottish coast immediately to the north of Edinburgh. Views to the north from George St or the castle reveal the firth with the hills of Fife beyond.

**Food:** Visitors to Edinburgh can look forward to sampling Aberdeen Angus beef, game and venison from the hills and moors, salmon and trout from the lochs and rivers, and of course seafood: lobster, prawns, crab, oysters, herring, haddock and cod. Traditional soups include cockieleekie (a broth of chicken, onion and leek), partan bree (a creamy crab soup) and Cullen skink (made with smoked haddock, milk, onion and potato). Loch Fyne kippers (smoked herring) are a popular breakfast dish, or you could try an Arbroath smokie (haddock smoked over birch/oak twigs) or Finnan haddie (haddock smoked over peat). Scottish salmon is famed worldwide and is equally delicious poached, baked or smoked. A main course of beef, lamb or venison might be followed by a dessert based on Scottish fruit (e.g. raspberries, gooseberies or rhubarb) or a dish of Atholl brose, a rich blend of cream, whisky and oatmeal. Snacks include Forfar bridies (pastry parcels filled with minced meat and vegetables) or stovies (a hash of potatoes, onions, cabbage and meat). And of course there is haggis. This famous Scottish dish uses the minced liver, heart and lungs of a sheep, mixed with oatmeal, onion, suet and seasoning. The mixture is used to stuff a sheep's stomach-bag, which is cooked by boiling or roasting. It tastes much better than it sounds! It is traditionally served with 'bashed neeps and chappit tatties' (mashed turnip and potato) on Burns Night (25 Jan.), St. Andrew's Day (30 Nov.) and Hogmanay (31 Dec.).

**Forth Road & Rail Bridges:** This pair of spectacular bridges spans the Firth of Forth (see **A-Z**) at Queensferry, about 8 miles west of the city. A ferry had plied the water here for over 900 years until, in 1890, the rail bridge was completed at a cost of £3.2 million. At the time it was the largest steel structure in the world; 54,000 tons of steel were used in its construction. Today it is the world's largest floodlit structure. The neighbouring road bridge opened in 1964. It stretches 1.4 miles across the Forth and cost £19.4 million. Its 500 ft towers support two steel cables, each 6 ft thick, from which a four-lane highway and a cycle/footpath are suspended. See **EXCURSIONS 1, 3 & 5**.

**Gladstone's Land:** This six-storey tenement building dates from 1617 and has been restored and furnished in the style of a 17thC Old Town (see **A-Z**) house. 1000-1700 Mon.-Sat., 1400-1700 Sun. (April-Oct.); £2, child £1. See **WALK 1**.

**Grassmarket:** A street in the Old Town (see **A-Z**), below the castle, where weekly markets were held. It was also the setting for public executions: the site of the gallows is marked by a cross in the small garden at the east end. The 18thC White Hart Inn, on the north side, was frequented by Highland drovers who brought their cattle here to market, and was visited by Robert Burns (see **A-Z**) and William Wordsworth.

**Greyfriars Bobby:** Bobby was a terrier belonging to Jock Gray, a local shepherd. When Jock died in 1858, the dog stayed at his grave side in Greyfriars Kirkyard every day for 14 years. He became so popular that a statue of him was erected in 1873, after his death. The statue is opposite the gates of Greyfriars Kirkyard (corner of George IV Bridge and Candlemaker Row). Bobby's gravestone can be seen inside the kirkyard gates, and his collar and bowl are in Huntly House Museum (see **ART GALLERIES & MUSEUMS**).

**Haymarket:** Edinburgh's second main-line railway station. It is not a terminus, merely a stop on the main line west to Glasgow and London Euston, four minutes from Edinburgh Waverley. It is more convenient for people staying in the West End of the city.

**Heart of Midlothian:** On the south side of the Royal Mile (see **A-Z**), just to the west of St. Giles' Cathedral (see **A-Z**), this heart-shaped pattern of cobblestones set into the road marks the site of the condemned cell within the Old Tolbooth, once the notorious town prison. It was demolished in 1817 but brass plates in the road mark its original outline. The old custom of spitting on the heart for good luck persists to the present day. See **WALK 1**.

**Holyroodhouse, Palace of:** The palace is the royal family's official Scottish residence. It was founded in the late 15thC by James IV and probably had its origins in the guest-quarters attached to the neighbouring 12thC Abbey of Holyrood (the abbey ruins lie behind the present-day palace). The palace, which was extensively rebuilt and expanded in the 17thC, has close links with Mary, Queen of Scots, who lived there from 1564-70, through the troubled years of the murder of her secretary Rizzio in 1556, and the death of her husband Lord Darnley in 1567. Rizzio was stabbed to death in one of Mary's rooms by her jealous husband and his accomplices; a brass plaque in the floor

Holyroodhouse

marks the spot where he fell. Bonnie Prince Charlie stayed here during the Jacobite uprising of 1745 and George IV used the palace during his historic visit in 1822. It was at King George's behest that the palace was refurbished, and renovation and restoration continued over the next hundred years. Most of the palace is open to public view (except when the queen is in residence), including the Throne Room, Drawing Rooms, the sumptuous King's Bedchamber, the Picture Gallery, and Lord Darnley's and Mary's rooms. Guided tours only 0930-1715 Mon.-Sat., 1030-1630 Sun. (April-Sep.); 0930-1545 Mon.-Sat. (Oct.-Mar.). Tours start every 15 min in summer and last 35 min.; £2.35, child £1.10. See **WALK 1**.

**John Knox House:** 45 High St, Royal Mile. This interesting house dates from the early 16thC, though Knox (see **A-Z**) probably lived here only for the few months prior to his death. The museum inside houses many exhibits associated with the life of the great reformer and preserves many original features of the building, including a fireplace and a 16thC wall-painting. 1000-1700 Mon.-Sat. (April-Oct.), 1000-1600 Mon.-Sat. (Nov.-Mar.), last admission 1630/1530; £1.20, child 50p; Bus 1, 3, 6, 21, 31, 33, 34, 35, 80, 81, 82.

**Knox, John (1505-72):** Born near Haddington, East Lothian, this 16thC leader of the Scottish Reformation was largely responsible for the establishment of the Protestant faith in Scotland. Originally a Roman Catholic priest, he committed himself to Protestantism in 1545, and was minister of St. Giles' Cathedral (see **A-Z**) from 1559 until his death. Although he is remembered principally for introducing the austere doctrines of Calvinism, thus setting the pattern of Scottish religious and social life over the following three centuries, he also bequeathed much valuable historical documentation to future generations. See **John Knox House**.

JOHN KNOX HOUSE

**Lady Stair's House:** Lady Stair's Close, Lawnmarket, Royal Mile. This house was built in 1622 and sold in 1719 to Elizabeth, Dowager Countess of Stair, from whom it takes its name. Following restoration in 1897, it was presented to the city in 1907, and today houses a literary museum dedicated to three great Scottish writers: Robert Burns (see **A-Z**), Sir Walter Scott (see **A-Z**) and Robert Louis Stevenson (see **A-Z**). 1000-1800 Mon.-Sat., 1400-1700 Sun. (during the Festival only); 1000-1700 Mon.-Sat. (Oct.-May); free. See **WALK 1**.

**Libraries:** The National Library of Scotland, George IV Bridge, tel: 2264531. Copyright library receiving a copy of everything published in the UK. Reference only. It has free exhibitions in the entrance hall. Central Library, George IV Bridge, tel: 2255584. Lending library.

**Meadows, The:** A pleasant area of parkland to the south of the city centre, on the site of a drained loch. The International Exhibition of Industry, Science and Art was held here in 1886; remnants include the entrance pillars at the west end of Melville Dr. and the whalebone arch at the end of Jawbone Walk. Today there are trees, paths, a cricket pitch, tennis courts and a children's playground.

The Meadows

**Military Tattoo:** This spectacular show is held annually on the Castle Esplanade (see **EDINBURGH CASTLE**) during the three weeks of the Edinburgh International Festival (see **A-Z**) in Aug. It is an exciting display of mock battles, fireworks, gymnastics, horsemanship, pageantry and massed pipe bands, and ends movingly with a lone, spotlit piper playing a farewell lament. For information contact the Tattoo Office, 22 Market St, tel: 2251188. Postal bookings are accepted from Jan. onward. Counter sales from the Ticket Centre, 5 Waverley Bridge, begin in early July and tickets cost £5-8.

**Mound, The:** This is the name given to the steep hill that winds down to Princes St (see **A-Z**) from the Royal Mile (see **A-Z**) between Lawnmarket and High St. It was created during the building of the New Town (see **A-Z**) by the dumping of rubble excavated from the foundations, with the intention of making a short cut from the Old Town (see **A-Z**) to the New across the boggy depression of the Nor' Loch (now fully drained and occupied by Princes St Gardens and the railway).

**Music:** Many kinds of music can be enjoyed in Edinburgh, from classical concerts in the Usher Hall to jazz bands playing in smoky pubs. The music most often associated with Scotland is pipe music, and the stirring strains of the massed pipe bands can be enjoyed at the Military Tattoo (see **A-Z**), and also at the Festival opening parade along Princes St. But don't miss out on Scottish folk music, which ranges from moving historical ballads to toe-tapping fiddle tunes. Ask at the Tourist Information Centre (see **Tourist Information**) or check the listings in *What's On, The List* and the local newspapers (see **What's On**). See **ENTERTAINMENT, NIGHTLIFE.**

**New Town:** Edinburgh's New Town is a masterpiece of late-18th and early-19thC urban planning, and today forms the largest urban conservation area in Britain. It was begun in the 1780s, after a proposal by George Drummond, Lord Provost of Edinburgh from 1725 to 1764, to ease the overcrowding in the squalid and crime-ridden Old Town (see **A-Z**) as the capital's population steadily increased. The street plan of the original New Town (the regular grid bounded by Queen St, Princes

St, St. Andrew Sq. and Charlotte Sq.) was designed by James Craig, an unknown, self-taught architect only 23 years old. The graceful Georgian terraces, with their regular three-by-four windows, channelled ashlar ground-floor walls, elaborate fanlights and black-painted wrought-iron lampposts and railings, attracted the city's upper classes, and such was the New Town's popularity that soon further developments were added, extending north and west as far as Stockbridge, and around the flanks of Calton Hill (see **A-Z**). Today the New Town is the financial and administrative heart of Edinburgh, with many buildings being sensitively converted to offices and banks. A larger number still remain as desirable private houses, meaning the New Town is also a community enjoying the best in elegant city centre living. See **CITY DISTRICTS**, **WALK 2**.

**Old Town:** The ancient heart of the city, built along the ridge stretching from the Castle Rock to Holyroodhouse (see **A-Z**). The Old Town probably began around the 7th or 8thC as a huddle of cottages close to the castle gates, which gradually spread down the ridge as Edinburgh gained importance as a strategic site. By 1376 the population had grown to 2000. A city wall was built after the Scottish defeat at Flodden in 1513, and pressure of space meant that houses were built upwards, resulting in the characteristic tall tenement buildings separated by narrow streets and closes. By the 18thC the population was 50,000 and there was much squalor and overcrowding, which led to the decision to build the New Town (see **A-Z**) to the north. Today, renovation has made the Old Town a pleasant place to live, and its atmospheric streets and alleyways are crammed with historic houses, museums, pubs, tearooms and many other attractions. See **CITY DISTRICTS**, **WALK 1**.

**One o'Clock Gun:** Every day this Edinburgh institution never fails to make the Princes St shoppers jump. The tradition of firing a cannon from the castle battlements at one o'clock began in 1848 to serve as a time signal for ships in the Firth of Forth (see **A-Z**). In addition, since 1861, the gun has been linked electrically to a time-ball on top of the Nelson Monument on Calton Hill (see **A-Z**); the ball drops on the stroke of one, thus giving a visual time signal.

**Parliament House & Law Courts:** Parliament Sq., High St, Royal Mile. A complex of buildings hidden behind an early-19thC neo-classical façade. One of these, Parliament House, was completed in 1639 at the order of Charles I and was the assembly place of the Scottish Parliament from that time until the Treaty of Union in 1707. It boasts a magnificent 17thC hammer-beam roof, and stained-glass windows depicting the inauguration of the Court of Session by James V in 1532. Today the hall and surrounding buildings are the home of the Scottish Law Courts. 0930-1630 Tue.-Fri.; free. See **WALK 1**.

**Pentland Hills:** This range of hills rises to 1600 ft immediately to the south of Edinburgh, offering pleasant walks and picnics within easy reach of the city. They are also the home of Hillend Ski Centre (see **SPORTS**), Britain's longest artificial ski slope. The chair lift at Hillend is also open to walkers.

**Princes Street:** One of the most famous and beautiful streets in the world. It dates from the construction of the New Town (see **A-Z**) in the late 18thC and is unusual in being built-up on one side only, allowing magnificent views across to the castle (see **Edinburgh Castle**) and the Old Town (see **A-Z**). It began life as an up-market residential street but today it is the city's main shopping thoroughfare.

Princes Street

**Princes Street Gardens:** The gardens were laid out in the early 19thC for the residents of Princes St in the newly-built New Town (see **A-Z**). They occupy the site of the Nor' Loch (North Loch) which lay beneath the Castle Rock (see **Edinburgh Castle**), and have been open to the public since 1850. Points of interest include the Ross Bandstand, where open-air concerts are held in summer; the Floral Clock beside the steps at the foot of The Mound (see **A-Z**); the Scott Monument (see **A-Z**); the Scottish-American War Memorial; and statues of explorer and missionary David Livingstone, and poet Allan Ramsay.

**Rose Street:** A pedestrian precinct running parallel to Princes St. At one time it was famous for its pubs and was known as the beer-drinker's golden mile but today many of the bars have lost their character and the street is no longer a classic 'pub-crawl'. The Abbotsford (see **PUBS**) and the Kenilworth are still worth a visit though.

**Royal Botanic Garden:** Inverleith Row. The history of Edinburgh's Botanic Garden dates back to 1670, making it the second-oldest in Britain after Oxford's. From its beginnings as a physic garden established by Edinburgh University's first Professor of Medicine on a small plot of land near to Holyrood Abbey (see **Holyroodhouse**), it was moved several times before arriving at its present 70 acre site in 1823. It now receives over 500,000 visitors each year and is only a 10 min bus ride from the city centre. It includes an exhibition hall, demonstration gardens, arboretum, peat garden, woodland garden, rock and heath garden, azalea lawn, alpine house and the largest collection of rhododendrons in the UK. 0900-1 hr before sunset Mon.-Sat., 1100-1 hr before sunset Sun. (Mar.-Oct.); closes at dusk Nov.-Feb.; free; Bus 8, 19, 23, 27, 39. See **WALK 4**.

**Royal Mile:** The narrow cobbled street that runs downhill from the castle (see **Edinburgh Castle**) entrance to the gates of Holyroodhouse (see **A-Z**) and forms the backbone of Edinburgh's Old Town (see **A-Z**). It is so named because it was the route followed by the royal carriages that conveyed kings and queens between the palace and the castle. See **WALK 1**.

Royal Mile

**St. Giles' Cathedral:** High St, Royal Mile. Strictly speaking, this church should be referred to as the High Kirk of Edinburgh. It was a cathedral proper only during the years 1633-38 and 1661-89, but the name has stuck. There has been a church on this site since AD 854 but most of the present-day structure dates from 1829-33, when the exterior was faced in smooth stone. The four central pillars within date from the 12thC, the choir from 1460 and the impressive crown spire from 1495. The ornate Gothic Thistle Chapel was added in 1909-11. The famous Reformer, John Knox (see **A-Z**), was minister here from 1559 until his death in 1572. 0900-1900 (1700 in winter) Mon.-Sat., later on Sun. Public worship: 1200 Mon.-Sat.; 0800, 1000, 1800, 2000 Sun. Admission to the kirk is free; to the Thistle Chapel 30p , child 5p; Bus 1, 6, 34, 35. See **WALK 1**.

**Salisbury Crags:** The impressive line of cliffs that rises above the city to the west of Arthur's Seat (see **A-Z**). An enjoyable walk, known as the Radical Road, runs along the foot of the cliffs. See **WALK 3.**

**Scotch Whisky Heritage Centre:** 358 Castlehill, Royal Mile. An exhibition with audio-visual displays and theatrical sets describing the industrial and social history of Scotch whisky, from its 17thC beginnings to the present day. 1000-1900 April-Oct., 0900-1700 Nov.-Mar.; £2.85, child £1.50; Bus 1, 6, 23, 27, 30, 34, 35, 40, 41, 42, 46, 89. See **WALK 1**.

**Scott Monument:** East Princes St Gardens. An elaborate Gothic spire towering 200ft above Princes St (see **A-Z**), built in 1840-46 as a memorial to one of Scotland's best-loved novelists, Sir Walter Scott (see **A-Z**). The ornate exterior includes carvings of characters from Scott's novels, and at the bottom is a 30-ton white marble statue of Scott with his dog, Maida. You can climb the 287 steps to the top and enjoy magnificent views of the city. It is normally open 0900-1500 Mon.-Sat., admission 45p, but at present is closed for restoration work.

**Scott, Sir Walter (1771-1832):** One of Scotland's most famous writers, Scott was born and educated in Edinburgh. He lived at 28

Castle St in the New Town (see **A-Z**) for 28 years, before moving to the country house of Abbotsford in the Borders. His works include the romantic poem *The Lady of the Lake*, and the novels *Ivanhoe* and *Rob Roy*. He is buried in Dryburgh Abbey, near Abbotsford. See **EXCURSION 2.**

**Stevenson, Robert Louis (1850-94):** This world-famous writer was born at 8 Howard Pl., opposite the Royal Botanic Garden (see **A-Z**), and lived for about 30 years at 17 Heriot Row in the New Town (see **A-Z**). He qualified as an advocate at Edinburgh University in 1867, but made his name as a writer with such works as *A Child's Garden of Verse, Treasure Island, Kidnapped* and *The Strange Case of Dr Jekyll and Mr Hyde*. He also wrote the words of the well-known *Skye Boat Song*. He died in Samoa, in the South Pacific, and is buried there.

**Talbot Rice Art Gallery:** Old College, South Bridge. Houses Edinburgh University's permanent art collection, including some notable 17thC Dutch paintings, and 16th and 17thC bronzes. 1000-1700 Mon.-Sat. ; free; Bus 3, 7, 8, 21, 31, 33, 80, 81, 82, 87, 89.

**University of Edinburgh:** Founded under the Royal Charter of James VI in 1583, Edinburgh's University is the sixth-oldest in Britain. Its original site on the corner of Chambers St and South Bridge is known as Old College, and now houses the Law Faculty. Other main sites are at George Sq. (Arts and Social Science); New College, on The Mound (Divinity); Teviot Pl. (Medicine) and Kings Buildings, West Mains Rd (Science). The university has 11,000 students and enjoys a world reputation for excellence in medicine and science. Famous graduates from the past include Charles Darwin, Arthur Conan Doyle, Sir Walter Scott (see **A-Z**) and Robert Louis Stevenson (see **A-Z**).

**Water of Leith:** This is the small river whose deep, wooded valley cuts through the heart of the city. See **WALK 4.**

**Waverley Market:** A modern, enclosed shopping arcade next to Waverley station (see **Railways**). The principal Tourist Information Centre (see **Tourist Information**) is situated at street level.

Scott Monument

I ♥ SF

English Spoken
American Understood.
POST CARDS 12P.
POST CARDS 12P.
EDINBURGH

**Accidents & Breakdowns:** If you are involved in an accident where no-one has been hurt, exchange your name, address and insurance details with the other driver and take the names and addresses of any witnesses. If there are any injuries the police must be notified and an ambulance called.

In the event of a breakdown, AA and RAC members can call a 24 hr breakdown service: AA, tel: 0800-887766; RAC, tel: 0800-828282. Garages in the city providing a 24 hr breakdown service include: Albion Road Garage, tel: 6612102; Lochend Motor Co., tel: 6616264 (day), 5546558 (night). Edinburgh offices of motoring organizations: Automobile Association, 18-22 Melville St, tel: 2253301; Royal Automobile Club, 35 Kinnaird Park, tel: 6571122.

See **Consulates**, **Driving**, **Emergency Numbers**.

**Accommodation:** Edinburgh offers a wide range of accommodation, from the humble bed and breakfast to the world-class luxury hotel. The Scottish Tourist Board (STB) has recently introduced a two-tier system of classifying hotels and guesthouses: the range of facilities available is indicated by the classification, ranging from one crown for basic accommodation to five crowns for a luxury suite; and the quality of service is shown by the grading, which can be 'Approved', 'Commended' or 'Highly Commended'.
Room prices must, by law, be prominently displayed. A double room with bath and breakfast in a hotel will cost £30-75; a double room in a B & B will cost £8-10.
A list of hotels (*Tourist Accommodation Register*) is available free from the Tourist Information & Accommodation Centre at Waverley Market. The centre also provides a year-round Advance Reservation Service (at least three weeks' notice required) and an on-the-spot Reservation Service during peak summer months. There are other accommodation centres at Waverley station and Edinburgh airport. It is not wise to arrive in Edinburgh during the Festival without having booked your accommodation in advance. See **Camping & Caravanning**, **Tourist Information**, **Youth Hostels**.

**Airport:** Edinburgh airport lies 6 miles west of the city, just off the main A 8 road to Glasgow. A regular 'Airporter' bus service runs between the terminal and Waverley Bridge in the city centre from 0720-2230; service every 30 min 0820-1620, less frequent at weekends; journey time approximately 30 min; cost £2.50. A taxi from the airport to the city centre costs about £9. Airport facilities include a Tourist Information & Accommodation Desk, tel: 031-3332167, bank, currency exchange, restaurant, buffet, two bars, duty-free shop, gift-shop, a qualified nurse and facilities for disabled travellers. When making enquiries, tel: 031-3331000 and ask for the Airport Information Desk.

**Baby-sitters:** Available from Bruntsfield Helping Hands Agency, 45 Barclay Pl., tel: 2281382/2282858. Many of the better hotels will provide a baby-sitting service. See CHILDREN, **Children**.

**Banks:** See **Currency**, **Money**, **Opening Times.**

**Best Buys:** Edinburgh abounds with shops selling good-quality Scottish goods. The most popular souvenirs include fine woollen knitwear, hand-woven tweed from the Hebrides and, of course, kilts and tartan skirts. Scottish crafts, such as ceramics and silver jewellery, are often good value. Scottish produce like smoked salmon and haggis can be delivered by mail order all over the world, while a tin of shortbread or a packet of oatcakes will not take up much room in your suitcase. Don't forget to take home a bottle or two of malt whisky! See **SHOPPING**.

**Bicycle Hire:** Bicycles can be hired from the New Bike Shop, located at 13-14 Lochrin Pl., Tollcross, tel: 2286333, at a cost of about £10 per day.

**Budget:**

| | |
|---|---|
| Lunch in a café or pub | £3-8 |
| Dinner, without wine, in restaurant | £6-20 |
| Pint of beer | £1.30 (approx.) |
| Glass of whisky | £1.10 (approx.) |
| Museum admission | Mostly free |

**Buses:** The main city bus network is run by Lothian Region Transport (LRT), whose head office is at 14 Queen St, tel: 5544494. For enquiries, maps and timetables go to the Ticket Centre, 5 Waverley Bridge, tel: 2253858. Their maroon-and-white buses cover most of the city. Most services run along Princes St and each bus stop shows the numbers of the bus services that halt there. Pay your fare to the driver as you board; carry plenty of small change, as only the exact fare is accepted (tell the driver your destination and he will tell you how much to pay; children under five travel free). Special tourist tickets giving unlimited bus travel for one to 13 days are available from the Ticket Centre. Between 30 May and 2 Sep. a special Tourist Shuttle (Bus 99) runs every 30 min Mon.-Fri. from Princes St, passing most of the major tourist attractions (flat fare 75p, child 40p).

The green-and-white buses of Eastern Scottish Omnibuses (St. Andrew Sq. bus station, tel: 5568464) serve the towns and villages around Edinburgh, and also cover a number of city routes.
Scottish Citylink (St. Andrew Sq. bus station, tel: 5575717) run blue-and-yellow coaches providing long-distance and inter-city services throughout Scotland and the UK, e.g. Edinburgh to Glasgow, 70 min, £4.20 return; Edinburgh to London, 9 hr, £24 return.
Open-top sightseeing buses operate at 15 min intervals all year round, leaving from Waverley Bridge and enabling visitors to alight at various attractions, including the castle, the Royal Mile and the Palace of Holyroodhouse; flat fare £4.50.

**Cameras & Photography:** Edinburgh is probably Britain's most photogenic city, so don't skimp on film! Most major brands of film are available in chemists, newsagents, department stores and souvenir shops. Note that there are usually restrictions on photography in museums and art galleries, so check at the reception desk before taking any snaps.

National Monument

**Camping & Caravanning:** The booklet *Scotland: Caravan and Camping Sites* is available from the STB (see **Tourist Information**). Two sites serving the city are: Drum Mohr Caravan Park, Levenhall, Musselburgh (to the east of the city), tel: 031-6656867: open Mar.-Oct., cost of pitch (caravan, motor-caravan or tent) £5 per night for two people (£5.50 July & Aug.), plus 50p for each extra person, electricity hook-up, £1 extra; Little France Caravan Park, 219 Old Dalkeith Rd, tel: 031-6644742: open April-Oct., cost of pitch £5-£7.

**Car Hire:** Most car-hire companies require that you be over 21, with at least 12 months' driving experience on a full licence. A cash deposit will be needed unless you are paying by credit card. Rates and systems of charging vary from company to company, so make sure you are aware of the full cost inclusive of insurance, VAT and any surcharges. Third-party insurance is compulsory; collision damage insurance is optional but recommended. Rates can range from £12 per day plus 6p a mile, to £120 per week unlimited mileage for a small car, to £200 per week with unlimited mileage for a family saloon. There are car-hire companies at the following places: Avis, Edinburgh Airport, tel: 031-3331866, and 100 Dalry Rd, tel: 3376363; Budget, 116 Polwarth Gardens, tel: 2286088; Godfrey Davis, Edinburgh Airport, tel: 031-3332588, and 24 East London St, tel: 6611252; Hertz, Edinburgh Airport, tel: 031-3331019, Waverley Station Rail-Drive, tel: 5568835, and 10 Picardy Pl., tel: 5568311. Other firms can be found in the *Yellow Pages* telephone directory.

**Chemists:** Chemists are generally open 0900-1730 Mon.-Sat. A rota system operates for late opening and each shop displays a list showing those chemists that will be open late that evening. The main city centre shop is Boots, 48 Shandwick Pl., tel: 2256757. Police stations will assist in filling an urgent prescription. In a medical emergency, dial 999 and ask for an ambulance. See **Health**.

**Children:** Edinburgh offers many activities for children, from building sand castles on Portobello Beach (see CITY DISTRICTS) to flying kites in Holyrood Park. There is an informative booklet, *Scotland For Children*, available from the STB (see **Tourist Information**). You should be aware that children are not generally welcome in pubs in the city, though some country inns may advertise 'family rooms'. See **CHILDREN**.

**Climate:** Edinburgh enjoys a much drier but much colder climate than Glasgow and the west of Scotland. The best months to visit are May and June, when it is least likely to rain, and many flowers and trees are in full bloom. Average temperatures are 4°C in winter, 7°C in spring, 15°C in summer and 7°C in autumn.

**Complaints:** If you have been overcharged, or have a complaint about a hotel, restaurant or other establishment, ask to see the owner or manager of the premises. If he or she is unable to settle the matter to your satisfaction, you can report the incident to the STB (see **Tourist Information**) or to the Consumer Advice Department of Lothian Regional Council, tel: 5535454.

**Consulates:**
Australia – Hobart House, 80 Hanover St, Edinburgh, tel: 2266271.
USA – 3 Regent Terr., Edinburgh, tel: 5568315.

**Conversion Chart:**

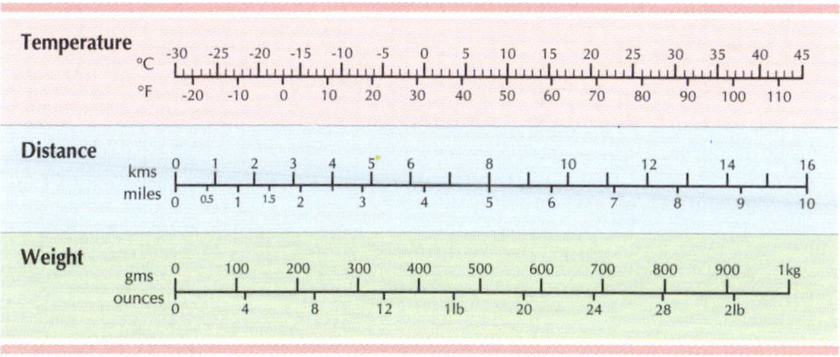


**Credit Cards:** See **Money**.

**Crime & Theft:** Crime in Edinburgh is low compared to many other capital cities, but you should still take precautions. Keep valuables in the hotel safe; take care of your wallet or handbag in crowded streets or shops; always lock your car and leave anything of value, such as a camera, out of sight in the boot. Report any thefts to the police immediately and if your passport is lost or stolen, contact your embassy or consulate (see **A-Z**). See **Emergency Numbers**, **Insurance**, **Police**.

**Currency:** The British unit of currency is the pound (£), equal to 100 pence (p). Banknotes come in denominations of £50 (red), £20 (purple), £10 (brown), £5 (blue) and £1 (green and Scotland only). The coins are £1, 50p, 20p, 10p, 5p, 2p and 1p. Scottish banknotes are occasionally refused in shops in England (though all, other than the £1, are legal tender) so change them for English notes before going south. See **Money**.

**Customs Allowances:**

| Duty Free Into: | Cigarettes | or Cigars | or Tobacco | Spirits | Wine |
|---|---|---|---|---|---|
| EC | 300 | 75 | 400 g | 1.5 *l* | 5 *l* |
| UK | 300 | 75 | 400 g | 1.5 *l* | 5 *l* |

**Disabled People:** Many places in Edinburgh have facilities for disabled visitors. For details, contact the Tourist Information Centre, Waverley Market (see **Tourist Information**).

**Drinks:** Scotland is world-famous for its whisky (the name comes from the Gaelic *uisge-beatha*, meaning 'water of life'). There are over 2000 brands of whisky to choose from. Over a hundred of these are

single malts, distilled purely from malted barley and aged in wooden casks, each as distinctive to the experienced palate as a classic wine. The rest are blends, mixtures of 15 to 50 grain whiskies (distilled from a mix of malted barley with other, unmalted, cereals), with a smaller amount of malt whiskies. Beers to look out for include Belhaven, Maclay's, Caledonian, Greenmantle and McEwan's 80/-. Beers are often classified in the traditional manner, as 60/-, 70/- or 80/- in order of increasing strength. These are roughly equivalent to English mild, bitter and best. Among non-alcoholic drinks, mineral water is becoming increasingly popular, and in addition to the usual French brands there are some Scottish waters, such as Highland Spring and Strathmore.

**Driving:** You will need your driving licence (foreign licences can be used in the UK for up to 12 months), and registration and insurance documents if you are bringing your own vehicle. Driving is on the left-hand side of the road. The wearing of seat belts is compulsory for the driver and front-seat passenger, as well as for back-seat passengers where seat belts are fitted. Road regulations are detailed in the booklet *The Highway Code*, available from the AA, RAC and many bookshops. Most road signs conform to international standards. Speed limits are 30 or 40 mph in built-up areas, 60 mph on single-carriageway main roads, and 70 mph on dual carriageways and motorways. Driving conditions are generally good. Driving in the city centre can be frustrating because of congestion, especially 0800-0900 and 1700-1800. The left-hand lane of many main streets is marked off by a solid white line. This lane is reserved for the use of buses only 0830-0915 and 1630-1800. See **Accidents & Breakdowns**, **Car Hire**, **Parking**, **Petrol**.

**Eating Out:** Edinburgh offers a wide range of cuisine, from traditional Scottish fare, through classic French, Italian and Chinese cooking, to Mexican and Thai. Many restaurants are concentrated in the city centre, especially in the New Town (see **A-Z**) and in the streets and closes along the Royal Mile (see **A-Z**).

Many less expensive eating places are to be found along Lothian Rd and in the Tollcross area, and outlets for fast food, such as pizza, kebabs, hamburgers and the traditional fish and chips, are widely distributed.

Lunch is generally served 1200-1400 and dinner 1900-2200. Some smaller Chinese and Indian restaurants serve food all day and stay open until after midnight, and a few Italian places in Lothian Rd stay open until 0300 or 0400.

*The Scotsman* and *Evening News* newspapers contain useful lists of restaurants. As a rough guide expect to pay £20 and over for an expensive meal, £10-20 for a moderately-priced one and under £10 for an inexpensive meal. See **RESTAURANTS 1 & 2**, **Food**.

St. Andrew Sq.

**Electricity:** Standard voltage is 240 V/50 Hz AC. Adaptors will be necessary for foreign appliances. Shaver sockets are international standard two-pin design, 240 V.

**Emergency Numbers:** To contact the police, fire brigade or an ambulance, tel: 999. On a payphone you can dial 999 without inserting any money. See **Crime & Theft**, **Police.**

**Events:** Full details of events in the city are available from the Tourist Information Centre at Waverley Market (see **Tourist Information**).
*25 January:* Burns Night, dinners and parties celebrating the anniversary of the birth of Scotland's best-known poet (see **Burns**).
*January-March:* International Rugby Union at Murrayfield Stadium.
*April:* Edinburgh Festival of Science & Technology; Edinburgh Folk Music Festival.
*June:* Royal Highland Agricultural Show at Ingliston Showground.
*August:* Edinburgh International Festival (see **A-Z**); Festival Fringe (see **A-Z**); Film Festival; Jazz Festival; Book Festival (biennial, next due 1993); Military Tattoo (see **A-Z**).
*31 December:* Hogmanay (New Year celebrations), crowds gather around the Tron Kirk (see **WALK 1**) to bring in the New Year.

**Guides:** Details of guided coach tours and walking tours in and around Edinburgh are available from the Tourist Information Centre at Waverley Market (see **Tourist Information**). If you would like to hire your own personal guide, contact the Scottish Tourist Guides Association, 25 Regents Terr., Edinburgh EH7 5BS, tel: 5574111.

**Health:** Overseas visitors are eligible for free emergency treatment under Britain's National Health Service at hospital Accident and Emergency departments, but you are strongly recommended to take out adequate medical insurance before your trip. EC nationals can take advantage of reciprocal health care arrangements by filling out the form E 111 before their trip. Contact your own health service for details.
In a medical emergency, tel: 999 and ask for an ambulance. There are 24 hr Accident and Emergency departments at the Royal Infirmary,

Lauriston Pl., tel: 2292477, and the Western General Hospital, Crewe Rd South, tel: 3322525. For less serious complaints, make an appointment to see a local doctor. Your hotel or the local police station will have a list of available doctors. For emergency dental treatment, contact the Edinburgh Dental Hospital, 31 Chambers St, tel: 2259511. See **Disabled People**, **Emergency Numbers**, **Insurance**.

**Insurance:** Overseas visitors are strongly advised to take out medical and travel insurance before departing. Your travel agent should be able to recommend a suitable policy. See **Crime & Theft**, **Driving**, **Health**.

**Laundries:** Most visitors will be content to use the service provided by their hotel, though it is usually faster and cheaper (about 1 hr, and £2-3 for a machine-load) to use one of the many coin-operated Launderettes to be found in the city. Centrally-located Launderettes are at 13 South Clerk St, 54 Elm Row and 7-11 East London St. There are dry-cleaners at 123 Hanover St, 23 Frederick St and 6 North Bridge.

**Lost Property Offices:**
Police Lost Property Office, Fettes Ave, tel: 3313141 (0900-1700 Mon.-Fri., 1800-2000 Mon. only).
British Rail Lost Property Office, Waverley station, tel: 5562477 (0830-1300, 1400-1700 Mon.-Thu.; 0830-1300, 1400-1630 Fri.; 0830-1200 Sat.).
Lothian Region Transport, 14 Queen St, tel: 5544494 and ask for the Lost Property Office (0900-1700 Mon.-Fri.).
Eastern Scottish Omnibuses, St. Andrew Sq. bus station, tel: 5568126 (0830-1230, 1330-1730 Mon.-Fri.).

**Money:** Banks are generally open 0930-1230, 1330-1530 Mon.-Fri. and 1630-1800 Thu. Many city centre banks remain open at lunchtime. The Clydesdale Bank at the Tourist Information Centre, Waverley Market, is open 0830-2030 Mon.-Sat., 1100-1500 Sun. and offers currency exchange facilities, as do a number of city centre banks. A number of English and overseas banks have a branch in the city: Barclays,

35 St. Andrew Sq.; Citibank, 2 Festival Sq.; Bank of America, 24 St. Andrew Sq.; First National Bank of Chicago, 46 Charlotte Sq. There are currency exchange bureaux at Waverley station and 23 Princes St. Traveller's cheques are widely accepted throughout Edinburgh and Scotland – you will need your passport when cashing them. It is best to exchange cheques and currency in a bank, as they offer better rates than hotels and exchange bureaux. Credit cards are widely accepted by hotels, restaurants, shops and car-hire companies – look for their signs in the window. The American Express office is at 139 Princes St, tel: 2257881 (0900-1700 Mon.-Fri., 0900-1200 Sat.).
Most goods and services in the UK are liable to 17.5% sales tax (called Value Added Tax or VAT). Foreign visitors may be able to reclaim this tax on any goods they buy, but the procedure is so cumbersome that it is only worthwhile for large purchases. The scheme is run only by certain large stores and speciality shops, whose staff will explain to you what you must do. See **Crime & Theft**, **Currency**.

**Newspapers:** As well as the full range of national British newspapers, you will find that Scotland has two quality national dailies of its own: *The Herald* and *The Scotsman*, and the weekly *Scotland on Sunday*. The last two are published in Edinburgh, as is the *Evening News*, a local Edinburgh paper containing much useful information on entertainment. Foreign newspapers and magazines are available from several city centre newsagents. Try John Menzies on Princes St or Charles Burns, 351 High St, Royal Mile (opposite St. Giles' Cathedral). See **What's On**.

**Nightlife:** Edinburgh's nightlife does not grind to a halt when the Festival ends. All year round there is a wide selection of nightclubs, discos, casinos and bars to entertain those night owls who enjoy revelling into the small hours. See **ENTERTAINMENT**, **NIGHTLIFE**.

**Opening Times:** In general:
Banks – 0930-1230, 1330-1530 Mon.-Fri. and 1630-1800 Thu. Some city centre and airport banks open longer hours and at weekends.

Offices – 0900-1700 Mon.-Fri.
Post offices – 0900-1730 Mon.-Fri., 0900-1230 Sat. Smaller offices may close for lunch 1230-1330.
Pubs – 1100-2300 Mon.-Sat., often with late opening until 2400 or 0100 Thu.-Sat. Some pubs close 1430-1700. On Sun. most pubs open 1200-1400, 1930-2300. A few will be open all day.
Shops – 0900-1730 Mon.-Sat. Some of the large shops on Princes St are open Sun.

**Orientation:** The city is clustered around the spine of the Royal Mile, which runs eastward from the castle to Holyroodhouse, below the prominent hill of Arthur's Seat. To the north of the castle is Princes St and the regular grid-pattern of the New Town. To the south of the castle, and extending along the Royal Mile, is the Old Town. Note that Edinburgh streets often change name several times. For example, the Royal Mile begins as Castlehill, then becomes Lawnmarket, High St, Canongate and Abbey Strand before it reaches Holyrood.

South Queensferry

**Parking:** There are city centre car parks at Castle Terr. (off Lothian Rd) and the St. James's Centre (east end of Princes St). There are parking meters on many streets. A single yellow line at the kerb means no parking during the daytime; a double yellow line means no parking at any time. Traffic wardens are plentiful and vigilant. Penalties for illegal parking range from a £16 fine to the towing away and impounding of the vehicle. See **Driving**.

**Passports & Customs:** On arrival in the UK you will need a valid passport. No visas are necessary for EC citizens, Commonwealth citizens (including Australia, Canada and New Zealand), citizens of the USA or the Republic of South Africa.
At customs, on entering the country, if you have goods to declare over and above your duty-free allowances you should go through the 'Red Channel' (you must also declare anything you intend to leave or sell in the UK); if you have nothing to declare you should follow the 'Green Channel' (which is subject to spot checks by customs officers). There are no restrictions on the amount of money you may take into or out of the country. See **Customs Allowances**.

**Petrol:** Petrol is widely available and unleaded petrol is indicated by a green sign. Many stations are self-service. There is a 24 hr petrol station at Links service station, 21-27 Barclay Pl., Tollcross. See **Driving.**

**Police:** British police wear a dark-blue uniform, and peaked cap with a chequered band. They are not armed and you will generally find them friendly and helpful in their dealings with visitors. In an emergency, dial 999 and ask for the police. Police Headquarters in Edinburgh is at Fettes Ave, tel: 3313131. See **Crime & Theft**.

**Post Offices:** These are indicated by a red sign with yellow lettering. Letter boxes are painted bright red and display times of collections. Post offices sell stamps for letters and parcels, and there is often a vending machine outside which will sell stamps when the office is closed. Within the UK, letters can be sent either first or second class: first class is slightly more expensive but should guarantee next-day delivery;

second-class mail may take several days to arrive. Letters up to 60 g within the UK or up to 20 g within the EC cost 24p, and for the rest of Europe letters up to 20 g cost 26p. Airmail letters up to 10 g, to the rest of the world, cost 37p while aerogrammes cost 32p.
The Head Post Office is at 2-4 Waterloo Pl., EH1 1AA (0830-1800 Mon.-Fri., 0830-1230 Sat.). You can receive mail addressed c/o Poste Restante here, though you will need your passport or other identification when you go to collect it. See **Opening Times**.

**Public Holidays:** 1 Jan. (New Year's Day); 2 Jan. (Bank Holiday); Good Fri.; Spring Bank Holiday (May); August Bank Holiday; 25 Dec. (Christmas Day); 26 Dec. (Bank Holiday). Bank holidays are usually only observed by banks, and most shops and offices remain open.

Royal Botanic Gardens

**Railways:** All local and inter-city rail services depart from Waverley station, situated towards the east end of Princes St. (see **A-Z**). First-class and standard-class tickets are available, and special reductions are offered on certain routes. There are frequent and fast services from Edinburgh to London Kings Cross (5 hr). The standard fare is £64; Supersaver tickets (not valid for travel on Fri. and certain Bank Holidays) cost £54 return; an Apex ticket (limited availability, must be booked at least seven days in advance) costs £44 return. Edinburgh to Glasgow costs £5 single, £6.20 cheap day return. There are also regular services to Perth, Dundee, Aberdeen and Inverness. Special tourist tickets offering cut-price travel on trains, buses and ferries in the Scottish Highlands and Islands are also available. For rail information and timetable enquiries, tel: 031-5562451. There is also a helpful Information Desk in Waverley station.

**Religious Services:** To find out details of times and places of worship for a variety of religious denominations, contact the Tourist Information Centre at Waverley Market (see **Tourist Information**).

**Sports:** The most popular spectator sport in Scotland is Association Football (soccer). Edinburgh has two major teams, Heart of Midlothian FC and Hibernian FC. There are regular Sat. and Wed. matches in season (winter) at their respective grounds: Tynecastle (off Gorgie Rd) and Easter Road (north of London Rd). Rugby union is played at Murrayfield stadium (off Corstorphine Rd), which hosts matches in the annual Five Nations international competition (see **Events**). There are occasional national and international athletics meets at Meadowbank stadium, London Rd, motor racing at Ingliston racetrack (west of the city) and horse racing at Musselburgh (east of the city). See **SPORTS**.

**Students:** Bring your International Student Identity Card – it will allow you to claim discounts on certain kinds of bus and rail travel, and on admission to certain museums, exhibitions, etc. Your university union may have reciprocal rights with those of Edinburgh and Heriot-Watt universities, in which case you will be able to use their facilities, including inexpensive cafeterias, bars, showers, TV lounges, etc. Edinburgh University unions are at Teviot Row, Bristo Sq.; Chambers St; and Kings Buildings, West Mains Rd. Heriot Watt University Union is at 23 Grindlay St.

**Taxis:** Like London, Edinburgh's taxis are distinctive black 'Hackney carriages'. The yellow 'For Hire' sign on the roof is lit when the cab is available. They can be hailed in the street, ordered by telephone or found at one of the many taxi ranks throughout the city centre. The main ranks are at Waverley station (where there are often long queues), Haymarket station, the West End, St. Andrew Sq. bus station and most of the side streets off Princes St. It can be very difficult to find a taxi during Fri. and Sat. evenings. Basic charge of 90p, plus 10p for every 345 yd (equivalent to around 50p per mile). Telephone numbers of 24 hr radio taxis: Castle Cabs 2282555; Central Radio Taxis 2295221; City Cabs 2281211. See **Tipping**.

**Telephones & Telegrams:** Public payphones are common throughout the city. The older blue payphones accept 2p, 10p and 50p coins, while the more modern, single-slot machines, which are replac-

ing the older ones, accept all coins except 1p. Instructions for use are clearly displayed in the phone booth. You can make local, long-distance and international calls from all telephones, either dialling direct or through the operator (UK operator, dial 100; international operator 155). Telephones with a green 'Phonecard' sign can only be used with a plastic card available from post offices and newsagents in £1, £5 and £10 versions. In the UK a 'collect' call is known as a reverse-charge call. To make an international call, dial 010 followed by the country code (USA and Canada 1, Australia 61, New Zealand 64, France 33, West Germany 49), then the area code, minus the initial zero, and the number. Full instructions can be found in any telephone directory. A wide selection of overseas directories can be consulted in the reference department of the Central Library (see **Libraries**).
The cheapest time to make UK calls is 1800-0600 weekdays, and during the weekend. Local calls cost around 10p for 3 min. The cost of a 3 min call to London is 30p; USA £2; France and Germany £1.10; Australia £3.
All telegrams must be dictated by telephone; there is no longer a traditional counter service. Dial 100 and ask for Telemessage (for UK and USA) or International Telegrams (rest of world).

**Time Difference:** The British Isles use Greenwich Mean Time from late Oct. to late Mar. and then change to British Summer Time (GMT plus 1 hr).

**Tipping:** Hotels and restaurants often include a service charge in your bill. Where service is not included, it is customary to leave a tip of 10-15% to waiting staff. A porter gets 30-50p per bag. Taxi drivers often get 10-15% of the fare, and hairdressers 10% of the bill. Tipping is not expected in theatres, cinemas and petrol stations.

**Toilets:** In the city centre there are public toilets at: Canongate, Royal Mile; Castle Terr. car park; Haymarket; corner of The Mound and Princes St; St. James's Centre; Waverley Market; Ross Bandstand, Princes St Gardens. The Superloo in Waverley station has showers and shaving points in addition to normal toilet facilities.

**Tourist Information:** The main source of information and advice for visitors to the city is the Tourist Information and Accommodation Centre at Waverley Market, Princes St, tel: 5571700. It includes an accommodation reservation service and a bank with currency exchange facilities. 0830-2000 Mon.-Sat., 1100-2000 Sun. (open daily until 2100 July & Aug.). There is another Tourist Information Office at Edinburgh Airport.
The Scottish Travel Centre, South St. Andrew St, tel: 3322433, is open the same hours as the Tourist Information Centre and provides information and advice on travel and tourism in the rest of Scotland, including tours and excursions.
The Scottish Tourist Board is at 23 Ravelston Terr., Edinburgh EH4 3EU, tel: 3432433. Postal and telephone enquiries only. It can provide information on all aspects of tourism in Scotland. The STB has a London office at 19 Cockspur Rd, London SW1Y 5BL, tel: 071-9308661. See **Guides**, **What's On**.

**Transport:** Edinburgh is a fairly small city with a compact central area where most of the major attractions are concentrated. It is probably best explored on foot. For longer trips within the city, use the efficient bus system (see **Buses**). For destinations outside Edinburgh, you can use either the bus or train. The latter is usually faster and more comfortable, but also more expensive. See **Airport**, **Railways**, **Taxis**.

**Traveller's Cheques:** See **Money**.

**What's On:** To find out what's happening on the city's entertainment scene, consult the following publications: *What's On In Edinburgh*, a free monthly booklet, available from the Tourist Information Centre (see **Tourist Information**), lists current events, exhibitions and entertainment; *The List*, a fortnightly magazine, available from newsagents, contains detailed lists of events and entertainments in Glasgow and Edinburgh – cinema, theatre, music, art, rock, sport; the *Evening News* is a local newspaper with a useful restaurants and entertainment section. It is published daily Mon.-Sat. and is available from newsagents and street vendors. See **Events**, **Newspapers**.

**Youth Hostels:** The Scottish Youth Hostels Association has two hostels in Edinburgh, which are open to visitors with a national or international membership card: Bruntsfield, 7 Bruntsfield Cres., tel: 4472994, and Eglinton, 18 Eglinton Cres., tel: 3371120. There is an Independent Hostel at 8 Blackfriars St, tel: 5573984. It is self-catering (with free use of the kitchen) and has hot showers. No membership is needed to stay here. It is open 0630-0230 and costs £4.50 per night. There is also a YMCA in Princes St, tel: 2251174, and a YWCA at Randolph Cres., tel: 2254379.

This book was produced using QuarkXPress™
and Adobe Illustrator™ on Apple Macintosh™
computers and output to separated film
on a Linotronic™ 300 Imagesetter

*Text:* Neil Wilson
*Photography:* Keith Allardyce and Bob Wood
*Electronic Cartography:* Susan Harvey Design

First published 1990 Second Edition 1992
Reprinted 1994

Published by HarperCollins Publishers
Printed in Italy by Amadeus S.p.A.
ISBN 0 00 470020-1

Guidebook information is subject to being outdated by changes to opening hours, prices, and by fluctuating restaurant standards. Every effort has been made to give you an up-to-date text but the publishers cannot accept any liability for errors, omissions or changes in detail or for any consequences arising from the use of information contained herein. The publishers welcome corrections and suggestions from readers; write to:
The Publishing Manager, Travel Guides,
HarperCollins Publishers, PO Box,
Glasgow G4 0NB.